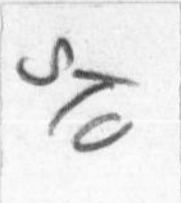

6-19-74

Trade and Investment Policies In the Americas

A JNO. E. OWENS MEMORIAL FOUNDATION PUBLICATION

Trade and Investment Policies In the Americas

EDITED BY STEPHEN E. GUISINGER

SOUTHERN METHODIST UNIVERSITY PRESS • DALLAS

Library of Congress Catalog Card Number: 73-84723
ISBN: 0-87074-136-5

Contents

Introduction

ON AUGUST 15, 1971, the government of the United States announced a series of changes in its foreign economic policies that caught the rest of the world by surprise. In the time following these policy changes, an interim agreement among the major developed countries on exchange rate parities has been reached, the U.S. import surcharge has been dropped, the process for rebuilding the international monetary system has been set in motion, and the United States balance of payments continues to record deficits. While the specific effects of the policies adopted on August 15 can be endlessly debated, it is important to recognize that these changes in U.S. policy were very consciously founded on a "new reality" in the world economy—that national economies, especially those of the developed countries, are closely linked as a result of the ease with which commodities and factors of production move among them. At the time of the policy changes, the United States argued that its deficit in the balance of payments was not solely, nor even mainly, the result of misguided American policies, but rather the inevitable consequence of policy decisions taken by the United States' trading partners. Thus, to an important extent, policy changes adopted on August 15 were not designed so much to correct our own policies as to induce other countries to change theirs. In defending the August 15 policies, the United States maintained that a permanent solution to the world's recurring monetary ills could only be reached when every nation recognized that its own economic policies could have serious repercussions abroad which could no longer be ignored. The irony of this position was clearly not lost on either the Mexicans or the Canadians, whose own economies were severely jolted by the United States' actions. And other nations were clearly puzzled as to how the unannounced, unilateral actions of the United States were meant to pave the way for international cooperation based on mutual trust.

Admittedly, with regard to international financial policies, the United States was eager to emphasize mutual responsibilities and to soft-pedal its own past mistakes; but the central role which the United States gave to the critical interdependence among nations in framing its own policies was a very accurate assessment of one of the most important, but generally least recognized, evolutions in the state of the world's economy over the past fifty years. From the beginning, trade has served to link nations together; but the extent to which national economies have become integrated in the last two decades is only beginning to be appreciated. Since the end of World War II, barriers to trade have declined dramatically in all the major developed nations: tariff levels have fallen and technological advances in transportation and communication have shrunk the economic distance between nations. One important contributor to this growing integration has been the multinational corporation, which by coordinating production and marketing decisions of its subsidiaries in several countries has effectively merged separate national markets into a single international market.

For all countries, however, international economic integration is a mixed blessing. A nation gains from increased trade but only at some sacrifice of its sovereignty and freedom of action. One nation cannot entirely insulate itself from the world economy, as disturbances in one part of the system tend to diffuse rapidly to other parts. Any one nation which attempts to improve its own welfare at the expense of others often finds that retaliation is swift and that the new equilibrium is no better and sometimes even worse than the old. These attributes of the interdependent world economy—the possibility of outside disturbances to the domestic economy, the speed with which patterns of trade change, the "unfair" policies adopted by other nations—all create tensions among nations which, unless they are clearly understood, can eventually destroy the benefits which interdependence brings to the world.

The problems and consequences of increased economic interdependence form one of the two themes which the essays in this volume share. The second is that these essays all treat some aspect of the trade policies employed by the countries of North and South America. The paper by Carlos Díaz-Alejandro deals with one important manifestation of international economic integration, namely the rapid rise in overseas investment and particularly the direct investments made by multinational corporations in developing countries. Díaz observes that investing and host countries frequently clash over the rights and responsibilities of the foreign investor, and all too frequently these conflicts are based on misconceptions on the part of both parties. The source of these misconceptions can be traced to the dual objectives of increased economic growth and increased national autonomy which developing countries wish to pursue simultaneously.

Foreign direct investment can promote rapid growth by bringing technical and managerial skills to the developing country and by opening up new areas of export that yield much needed foreign exchange. But these gains may occur only at the cost of loss of national control. The efforts of developing countries to reconcile these two objectives by stipulating the form, the duration, and even the permissible industrial sectors for direct foreign investment are frequently misconstrued by developed countries as arrant nationalism, when in fact these controls are exacting the best possible terms for the host country from its capital imports, assuring that the social returns of these investments exceed their social costs. Certainly, not every restriction placed on foreign capital in Latin America is the product of a finely calculated measure of social profitability; but the efforts of developing countries to maximize their gains from the exchange of goods and factors of production—particularly the nationalizations, expropriations, and renegotiated contracts between government and businesses—cannot be dismissed out of hand as misguided exercises of power.

The dual objectives of economic development and independence in Latin American countries are also analyzed in the paper by Joseph Grunwald, where he suggests that economic unions, such as the Latin American Free Trade Association (LAFTA), offer perhaps the most efficient and practicable strategy to achieve those dual objectives. Grunwald argues that the economic rationale for such integrative movements—namely, the cost savings achieved by greater specialization and the exploitation of scale economies—is sound and that the LAFTA members are equally committed to achieving integration. But an important barrier to progress so far has been the effects of the United States' tradition of bilateralism in its relations with LAFTA member nations. Instead of explicitly recognizing the associated states as a group, the United States has continued to develop its relations with each member separately, thus retarding the natural momentum toward regional integration. The effects of this bilateral foreign policy may in fact run counter to the United States' long-term interests, Grunwald suggests, since the rapid economic development of Latin America and the lowering of intraregional trade barriers would ultimately serve the United States' foreign policy objectives by minimizing the need for U.S. foreign aid to LAFTA nations and by strengthening the Latin American economies to the point where their barriers to U.S. imports would no longer be necessary. Specifically, Grunwald recommends that the United States should underline its commitment to LAFTA by offering trade preferences and foreign aid that are made contingent on progress toward integration. To the charge that this change in U.S. foreign policy would represent intervention in Latin American internal affairs, Grunwald would reply that the only benefits to the United States would come from the rapid economic development which is already an expressed goal of LAFTA members. Moreover, and perhaps most importantly, the intransigent bilateralism of the United States is itself a wrong kind of interventionism because it impedes the latent integrative forces within Latin America.

In his essay, Daniel Schydlowsky examines the ways in which the current trade policies of Latin American countries retard rather than promote rapid industrialization and economic development. Schydlowsky concludes that exports of manufactured goods can provide a vehicle for rapid growth in Latin America provided two conditions are met. First, other countries, particularly the developed countries, must be willing to accept increased imports of manufactured goods from Latin America. Second, the trade policies of Latin American countries must be altered to eliminate the implicit discrimination against exports. Latin American countries have not sought to promote manufactured exports because of what Schydlowsky terms the industrial inefficiency illusion—because of high import duties, the inputs into manufactured goods are high cost, and because of the generally overvalued exchange rates in Latin American countries, the returns to exports are low. With low earnings and high costs, manufactured exports give the illusion of being inefficiently produced even when the real factor costs and industrial technologies used are equivalent to those in developed countries. Schydlowsky recommends that the currently underutilized industrial capacity be used to produce for the export market. Various government policies must be altered to achieve this goal, including the subsidization of exports, the elimination of various hidden taxes on the multiple-use of industrial machinery, and the provision of the scarce resources, such as foreign exchange and working capital, needed to expand production.

The final paper in the volume is the keynote address of the conference which was delivered by Dr. Antonio Carillo-Flores. Drawing upon his experience as one of the principal architects of Mexican economic policy for the past two decades, Carillo-Flores surveys the current state of Latin American development and the ways in which trade policies of both the developed and developing countries in the Western hemisphere can contribute to more rapid economic growth. One very desirable policy change, according to Carillo-Flores, would be the preferential entry of manufactured exports from developing countries into the markets of the developed countries.

The Conference on Trade Policies in the Americas and the publication of this volume have been made possible by the Jno. E. Owens Memorial Lecture Committee. Jno. E. Owens, a prominent Dallas banker, was an advocate of more liberal trade policies and closer economic ties among nations. In a speech delivered in 1942 Mr. Owens said:

> When we go to South America and talk of the "Good Neighbor Policy," when such great conferences as we have had at Lima and Rio de Janeiro are held, the dominant note is the brotherhood of man. Unless we translate this into a free interchange of goods, there will be no lasting tie. . . . If we can come to believe that it is an ineluctable fact that trade means traffic and that traffic means an interchange of goods, then we will have accepted a virtue that will save the world for peace and plenty, for eternal hope and progress.

As the papers in this volume reveal, Jno. E. Owens's assessment of the foundations of peace and prosperity in the Western hemisphere is no less true today than it was in 1942.

STEPHEN GUISINGER

Southern Methodist University
June 5, 1973

Trade and Investment Policies In the Americas

CARLOS F. DIAZ-ALEJANDRO

The Future of Direct Foreign Investment in Latin America

INTRODUCTION: SOME OBVIOUS POINTS

The topic of foreign investment in Latin America is so fraught with misunderstandings and emotional overtones that it seems wise to start with some generalizations on which agreement is almost assured.

Latin American policies toward direct foreign private investment (DFI) arise, at a given point in time, mainly from the interplay of circumstances in the world economy with a given Latin American country's needs at its stage of development. The historical experiences of each country will also weigh heavily on the host country's perception of benefits and costs of foreign investment.

A key feature of the world economy of the 1960s was the existence of several major centers of capital and modern technology, such as the United States, Western Europe, Japan, and Eastern Europe. This situation opened the way for a gradual breakup of old commercial "spheres of influence" and the creation of a competitive and multilateral world trading community. Recent difficulties in the world monetary system show that there are important adjustment problems on the road to that free-trading, multilateral goal. Furthermore, the very rapid expansion of large multinational corporations (MNCs) could, in a few years, turn that relatively competitive world market into one dominated by a handful of oligopolies, controlling both finance and trade. One cannot dismiss a priori either the possibility that the 1970s may witness a return toward protectionist neo-mercantilism or the scenario in which an expanding world economy is managed from a few boardrooms located in New York, London, and Tokyo.[1] But I still find more likely an extension into the 1970s of the (on the whole) healthy 1960s competitive trends in world commerce and finance.

For Latin America, of course, this would be very fine indeed. The major Latin American countries are entering fairly sophisticated stages of industrialization, not very far behind those of Italy, Spain, and Eastern Europe, at which point selected foreign technology to assist in specific activities can be most helpful. The more potential suppliers of that technology there are, the better.

Most Latin American countries are also keenly aware of their need to expand and develop new, or nontraditional, export lines, a task which would be difficult or impossible in a stagnated world economy, and costly in one dominated by few oligopsonistic buyers.

But besides the need for advanced technology and new export outlets, Latin American countries have kept alive their old aspiration to consolidate their political and cultural independence by exercising greater control over their economic life. Most of these countries are getting ready to join the Atlantic and world communities as full-fledged members, without the need of "special relationships" with hegemonic powers. Such a transition, of course, is not without at least short-term costs. Concessional aid, for example, may gradually become a thing of the past for the more advanced Latin American countries (although donor countries, regardless of Latin American decisions, may cut it off anyway). This more standoffish, businesslike attitude is what one could expect as Latin America approaches the per capita income levels of Southern Europe within a multilateral world economy. Note also how the traditional dependence of Latin American exports on the United States market has declined from an unusually high 49 percent of the total in 1952, to 42 percent in 1958, and to 34 percent in 1968.

One could go farther and put forth the hypothesis that when DFI, expressed as a percentage of the host country's total assets, or in host country per capita terms, reaches "high" levels, sharp and violent political reaction is very likely to be generated. Mexico in 1910, Cuba in 1959, and Canada (and Puerto Rico?) in 1971 experienced such reaction.

Under these circumstances, I expect that most Latin American countries will increasingly ask, not whether DFI is intrinsically "good" or "bad," but rather which investments fit better into the host country's needs and plans, and under what conditions one can obtain those investments. Few would argue with the proposition that DFI can, under certain circumstances, benefit both investors and host countries. Today we see some socialist countries of Eastern Europe expanding their agreements with foreign capitalistic firms, while the popular front government of Chile certainly has not closed the door to all DFI, as witnessed by its automobile policy.

But it is also true that DFI, under present Latin American conditions, will not automatically yield results favorable to the host country's development. As the Indians of both North and South America found out, and as Ragnar Nurkse stated: "Foreign business investment is not always a happy form of encounter between different civilizations."[2] Another distinguished economist noted that

> since private international capital movements are motivated by expected net private return, and since the relation of net private return to gross social return is heavily influenced by taxes and other governmental policies, there is no *a priori* reason for placing much confidence in the principle of freedom of private international capital movements as a guarantor of economic efficiency in the international allocation of world investment resources.[3]

In other words, if foreign investors can borrow from the host country's credit resources at interest rates which are often negative in real terms, make profits sheltered behind effective rates of protection which reach 100 percent and above, benefit from holidays and exemptions from import duties on their raw materials, and remit profits abroad at overvalued exchange rates, there may be doubts as to the net benefits which the host country receives from such an activity.

This may or may not be typical of a given country at a given time. But it warns us that in the area of DFI, whether one deals with its economics or its politics, there is a great need for careful empirical analysis and cool pragmatism. Contrary to the usual stereotype, emotionalism and false heroics on this issue are not limited to Latin Americans only.

SOME U.S. MISCONCEPTIONS REGARDING DFI IN LATIN AMERICA

With distressing frequency, U.S. publications (even hardnosed business publications) and commentators use a disturbing rhetoric when dealing with the topic of U.S. investments in Latin America. Latin American leaders who argue for some new restriction on DFI are quickly labeled "anti-foreign" or "anti-American," without giving the reader an idea whether the regulation makes sense or not, and whether the one-to-one association of a particular business with the U.S. national interest is justified. If these publications used the same standards to report U.S. economic news, one can imagine their editions after President Nixon's August 15th, 1971, speech. They would have run headlines of the following sort: "Xenophobic Republican Boss Announces Pearl Harbor in Reverse—Anti-European Steps Also Taken."

This may seem like an exaggeration. Yet, last May, the *New York Times* ran a story announcing that the Argentine government was reversing "its shrill policy of economic nationalism," and had ousted "the xenophobic Minister of Economy, Aldo Ferrer. . . ."[4] It so happens that Dr. Aldo Ferrer has a long and distinguished international career, particularly in inter-American institutions. As a senior adviser to the Inter-American Committee on the Alliance for Progress, he and that other well-known "xenophobe," Dr. Roberto Campos of Brazil, jointly wrote a paper on the role of foreign investment in Latin American development.[5]

Parts of the statements by the Council of the Americas on the new foreign investment code of the countries participating in the Andean Common Market represent another example of overreaction and purple rhetoric. They also contain threats which are worse than offensive—they are not credible. The vice-president and general counsel of ELTRA Corporation of New York stated in a recent article:

> . . . a sense of detachment could have prevented the Council of the Americas, representing major U.S. business interests in Latin America, from coming forth with the hasty and inaccurate statement that the "fade-out joint venture" formula is an "unworkable and unrealistic proposal on the basis that foreign investors do not invest to go out of business". There are any number of modalities of "doing business", and if U.S. businessmen cannot prove versatile, surely those from Western Europe and Japan will![6]

To this one could add that the symbolism of pictures showing Fiat trucks being produced in Ford's old assembly plant in Chile should not escape U.S. firms. More tangible is the fact that ten European and Japanese auto-makers recently answered Chile's call for bids to form partnerships, in which the Chilean government would own at least 51 percent of the equity.

New forecasts or threats of a "drying-up" of willingness to invest sound particularly hollow when one reads about new contracts of Occidental Petroleum Corporation and other *U.S.* investors (not to mention non-U.S. investors) with Peru, less than three years after the air was filled with the same warnings motivated by the Peruvan-I.P.C. quarrel. Perhaps private settlement of that dispute has been reached, but to the naked eye it looks as if Peru has backed down less than the investing community. Mexican history, of course, provides other similar examples.

But perhaps the most spectacular rhetorical fireworks belong not to the private but to the public sector. Latin Americans, who during 1969 read in the opening lines of the Rockefeller Report on the Americas that "we went to visit neighbors and found brothers," heard recently that high U.S. officials, presumably talking about those same neighbors, say that "we don't have any friends there anyway."[7]

It is not entirely clear why the topic of DFI arouses such strong emotions, not only in host countries but also in investor countries. It may arise partly from confusing foreign investment with pure foreign aid, in spite of the clear fact that DFI has to do with business, risk, and profit—not charity. Another possible reason for exasperation at measures which restrict DFI inflows into Latin America is summarized in the question: "How can a developing area, which is captial-poor, reject it?" The question, however, admits many answers. First, as mentioned earlier, the major contribution DFI can make to the present stage of development in most of the Latin American countries is not really as a supplier of capital or foreign exchange, but as a provider of specialized techniques and talents. Secondly, and more fundamentally, host countries should desire something more than an indiscriminate increase in the inflow of the packages of capital, technology, and skills associated with DFI. They should try to control, in particular, the allocation of such an inflow, as well as the conditions under which it is contracted, so that the social return of the investment to the host country will exceed its costs. Of course, these calculations are not always carefully done, but on principle we are back to the need to analyze each project and such factors as its contribution to the development of local technology and to better knowledge of marketing channels, its effects on local entrepreneurships, etc. Thirdly, even when there is a positive net return to the host country from a particular DFI project, that country may not allow it for the sake of minimizing foreign presence in its economy, or in some sector of it. Surely, this is a trade-off every sovereign country has a right to choose; in fact, not all members of the Western community have the same degree of openness to DFI, and this is no impediment to mutually profitable trade and other financial links.

One also reads in the United States other arguments regarding

DFI which dim rather than increase understanding. It is, for example, sometimes pointed out that, after all, total earnings of U.S. investments in Latin America have averaged only 12 percent of the book value of that investment, not an exploitative figure. (The data for these calculations are obtained from company balance sheets.) The percentage figure by itself casts very little light on DFI issues. We all know about accounting conventions; in particular, there is considerable worry in Latin America about overinvoicing of imports from headquarters to subsidiaries, especially in pharmaceuticals, royalty and patent payments, etc., as ways to decrease book profits in host countries and increase them at headquarters. In several countries some plants show year after year accounting losses, and yet headquarters makes further investments into them. The problems raised by intracorporate sales and pricing techniques are not, of course, limited to Latin American-U.S. relations; furthermore, they do not always work to the disadvantage of host countries, as appears to be the case with oil.[8] But the point is that one should not debase discussions regarding DFI's careless use of book profit rates.

Another line of thought I find mystifying is one which implies that those wishing to control DFI are only, or mainly, "elite groups," bent on increasing their own power and status, if necessary at the expense of the masses. No doubt those types exist in Latin America (and elsewhere). But even stretching the use of "elite groups" into the realm of tautologies, the argument will give a dangerously misleading impression of Latin American feeling on this issue. The Venezuelan and Chilean Congresses, both democratically elected and both encompassing many ideological groups, have recently passed with near unanimity laws which restrict foreign investment in oil and copper, respectively. One could say that everyone in Congress is a member of the "elite" and acts mainly to work out his own impulses and psychic needs. Does anyone really believe that?

If the "elite" hypothesis were correct, one would expect moves to broaden political participation to improve the investment climate. Such a move seems to be occurring in Argentina this year, and here is how it has been reported from Buenos Aires:

> For United States investors here, who have an estimated one billion dollars at stake, the news of the lifting of the ban on political activity last Thursday night has raised some gloomy prospects.
>
> There is hardly any banned-until-now political party that does not favor a sharper nationalist course at the expense of foreign interests.[9]

While the historical record of DFI is very much alive in the Latin American mind, it tends to be ignored or downplayed in the United States. It is inevitable that in social history the sins of the father will haunt even the innocent son, and a greater historical perspective on the part of U.S. observers could help them to take a more detached view of day-to-day DFI crises. U.S. publications are not incapable of taking such a detached and long-range view of DFI frictions between investors and host countries; I simply find them more perceptive and cool when dealing with, say, the relations between Koreans and Southeast Asians and Japan, or between Algeria and France, than those between Latin America and the United States. In fact, they can sound downright enthusiastic about Algerian and Asian reactions to the French and Japanese.[10]

If nothing else, the coexistence in time of many different ways "of doing business" should give us some perspective when we face Latin American changes in the rules of the game for DFI. From reading the U.S. press one gets the clear impression that the investment climate for foreign corporations is better in Rumania and Yugoslavia, and even in the USSR, than in most Latin American countries. At first, this sounds crazy. On second thought, it illustrates the simple point that in the field of DFI the direction of change often gets more attention than the average level of treatment. Rough guidelines with a gradual tendency to become softer seem to be preferred to weak ones tending erratically to get tougher. If this is so, in most of Latin America things will get worse for traditional United States investors before they get better for those willing to operate in the new climate.

SOME LATIN AMERICAN MISCONCEPTIONS REGARDING DFI

The case for closer control over DFI is not helped by fallacious or misleading arguments which one often hears from Latin American sources, or from those sympathetic to Latin American aspirations. The prize for confusion in this area has to go to the "decapitalization" or the "they-take-out-more-than-they-put-in" argument.

This argument compares the amounts of fresh DFI inflows for a given period with outflows for profit remittances, dividends, etc., generated by the stock of DFI established in the host country. The argument points out that the latter sums exceed the former for Latin America; the implication is that DFI is bad for the region, draining it of its surplus, and therefore the region would be better off without DFI.

This line of thought compares fresh investments with outflows generated by old investments, and says nothing about the allocation and output (or surplus-generation) of those investments. Suppose, for example, that in a given country accumulated DFI is $100 million and it is all located in the export sector producing every year $30 million of exports. Suppose further that during the last fifteen years no new DFI has come in, but profit remittances have amounted to $10 million per year. It will then be argued that the host country will have been "decapitalized" by $150 million during that period, and that profit remittances have exceeded the original investment. This is "bad."

Compare the above situation with another, in which for fifteen years new DFI has come in at a rate of $10 million every year, and no profit remittances have yet taken place. Presumably this is "good," even though the investments may all go to produce Coca-Cola and corn flakes, at domestic prices twice as high as those in the world market.

The point is that the often-given comparison of fresh DFI with profit outflows is useless in judging whether or not a given country is benefiting from DFI. If the rate of new DFI inflows is constant, and the rate of profit annually remitted abroad is positive, sooner or later outflows will exceed inflows. And if the period is made long enough, the sum of annual profits or interest on a given investment will always exceed the original sum put in, whether one talks about DFI or a personal savings account. This will happen in DFI, which may be, for other reasons, good, bad, or indifferent for host countries.

If the host country's economy is diagnosed as limited primarily by an acute foreign exchange constraint, the direct and indirect balance of payments effects of DFI, and not only inflow minus profit outflow, should be brought in, including its impact on exports and net import substitution, *both* measured at world market prices. But more generally, other economic effects will have to be taken into account, in a full benefit-cost analysis, in trying to assess how DFI will change the host economy. That a given project does or does not save or generate foreign exchange should not necessarily be a decisive reason to accept or reject the proposal. Benjamin I. Cohen noted that one should also be on guard against the danger that fresh DFI in export lines could create new enclaves of small net benefit to host economies.

Joint ventures have many features which are appealing to host countries, when compared with those of fully-owned subsidiaries of MNCs. But insistence that *all* DFI must come in the form of joint ventures can have significant costs, under present world market circumstances.[11] Some MNCs simply will not touch joint ventures and may be more interested in investing in industrialized countries (including Eastern Europe) than in bargaining with LDCs; this may not matter much when there are several potential investors in the field (GM/autos), or when the MNC main asset is a brand name of doubtful social product (Kelloggs), but can delay entrance into specialized fields (IBM/computers). Other MNCs may be persuaded to give in to joint ventures, especially when the host country has a large domestic market, but at the price of letting them charge the mixed offspring higher sums for technology from headquarters. Those MNCs also generally show less zeal in promoting exports from their joint ventures than from their fully-owned subsidiaries. Under the cover of good will, they use more local and less foreign credit, and their retained earnings are lower. Their contribution to local entrepreneurship can be more apparent than real if rigid rules encourage phony local partners, or induce them to draw on experienced ones. Finally, some foreign investors may quite eagerly seek joint ventures in the hope of obtaining favorable treatment in tax and other matters which can be very onerous to host economies. In short, willingness to enter into joint ventures will not necessarily separate "good" from "bad" MNCs from the host country viewpoint, and very rigid rules in this area can involve important opportunity costs, both because of what is kept out and of what comes in. But let me grant the difficulty in separating "very rigid rules" from "realistic rules of thumb."

In the Latin American ambiance it is tempting to believe every story putting the foreign investor in a bad light, and to support every scheme to reduce his profit. Yet clearly there are better and worse ways of doing the latter, from the viewpoint of the host country's welfare. As emphasized by Paul P. Streeten, higher wages for privileged workers of MNCs are less desirable in general than higher taxes which can benefit via public expenditures larger and less favored groups in the population. Foreign investors may become exasperated at a new charge against them: that they pay wages which are *too high*! But in fact the charge, which should be extended to host country labor policies, has some substance, especially in countries with a widespread unemployment problem. And, obviously, keeping facts straight is a precondition for sensible decision making. (Before 1959 it was widely believed in Cuba that foreign oil companies had actually discovered vast amounts of oil in the island, but their worldwide strategy led them to keep these discoveries secret, as reserves. Alas, the story now appears untrue.)

DOMESTIC LATIN AMERICAN NEEDS AND THEIR INFLUENCE ON POLICIES TOWARD DFI

Much experimentation is going on in Latin America regarding policies toward DFI. Brazil relies on public command of monetary, fiscal, and foreign exchange policies to control DFI, and uses "positive" incentives and measures to induce the opening up of closed companies, foreign and national, to public participation. The Andean countries, on the other hand, have adopted a code which calls for tighter regulations over DFI. Some of the smaller countries, devoid of much bargaining power, desperately try to induce inflows by "wide-open" policies, taking full-page ads in the *New York Times* which produce embarrassment to other Latin Americans. Cuba continues to have nothing to do with any DFI, following a spartan (but not laconic) style. There are, furthermore, numerous proposals on what to do about DFI. Even in a given Latin American country, the social, political, and economic needs are many and often conflicting, pushing policy toward DFI in different directions, and frequently in contrary ways for different sectors within the same country.

The felt need to control basic sectors of the economy will be enough to maintain the pressure to nationalize, one way or another, major foreign-owned activities in the field of traditional natural resources, especially when such activities are of key importance to the host country. As ex-President Eduardo Frei has recently put it:

> The degree of awareness and development reached by these nations has led them to feel that it is against their interests and their very identity to allow natural resources, which are essential to them either as raw materials for their industry or as prime export items in their economies to remain in foreign hands. Thus, the nationalization of these resources will be unavoidable. . . .[12]

Ever since the colonial powers plundered the mineral and natural resource wealth of Latin America, starting in the sixteenth century, Latin Americans have felt that they were not getting a large enough share of the pure rents generated by those God-given natural resources. Furthermore, and granting that the prices at which those resources may be sold in world markets may remain erratic, most countries do not wish to maintain a situation where one more (to them) exogenous force, the foreign corporation, can introduce decisions affecting their control of foreign exchange receipts, regarded as an elementary precondition to rational planning. Those feelings should not be impossible to understand in the United States, where Alaska wants to own and operate the oil pipeline which will dominate its economic life, where Puerto Rico is pressing copper corporations for more favorable deals, and where Montana legislators complain that Anaconda's New York leadership treats that state like a colony.

So every shift in bargaining power can be expected to be used by Latin American countries to push a little farther toward local control. Note how Venezuela, which fourteen years ago was "wide open" to DFI, has very skillfully used Middle East circumstances to gain a greater share of its oil and gas revenues, as well as greater control over that industry. The history of Chilean copper is another, more complex, example of this trend.

The production and marketing of certain natural resources, such as oil, copper, and aluminum, generate high gross profits which are the result of two separate influences: pure rents from rich natural deposits, and the oligopolistic control of the industry. As a first approximation, one may view the sharing of pure rents as a conflictive zero-sum game between host countries and foreign corporations; both countries and corporations, however, have a common interest in not allowing too much competition in the industry. Because of this and other reasons, one can expect that foreign companies will continue playing some role in the field. For example, although the Chilean copper situation is still unclear, Cerro Corporation may not only end up settling amicably with the Chilean government, but could also provide technical help to the nationalized copper mines of that country. But clearly, the days of the ninety-nine-year concessions are gone in most (but not all!) of Latin America.

If host countries feel confident that they can now run old export lines, based on natural resources, they are likely to welcome some foreign investment for the sake of expanding new or *nontraditional exports,* particularly in manufacturing, but not excluding agricultural activities or "new" natural resources, like timber or iron ore. (What is a new natural resource in one country may be an old one in another.) Over the long run Latin American countries, acting jointly if possible, would do well to devote resources to developing their own marketing channels and outlets, and picking up expertise in the sale of nontraditional exports. But that process may take some time, and in the meantime the ready-made facilities of MNCs for worldwide connections loom appealingly. It has already been reported, for example, that IBM was in 1969 the largest exporter of manufactured goods from both Argentina and Brazil. Even here, however, the bargaining will typically be tougher than it was sixty or twenty years ago; if nothing else, there are now more foreign investors who can be induced to bid for export projects, as the Monroe Doctrine carries over less and less to economic matters.

There is a danger in too close a linkup between new Latin American exports and DFI. Investing countries may be tempted to condition access to their markets to favorable (discriminatory) treatment to their investors in exporting host countries. This is one reason among many why a system of hemispheric preferences would be far inferior to a generalized trade preference scheme. (It is hard to visualize Japanese-Latin American joint ventures tapping much of the U.S. market under hemispheric preferences.) And I would add that it is also inferior to just freezing trade restrictions at their pre-August 15, 1971 levels. Latin America has too much to gain, both economically and politically, from a nondiscriminatory world trading community, to toss away multilateralism for the sake of some short-term advantage.

It is known that the process of *import substitution* has been rather disorderly in most Latin American countries. In some sectors duplication of plant facilities behind excessive protection has led to unused capacity, inefficiency, and high costs. Often, as in automobiles and other durable consumer goods, foreign investors are conspicuously present and have not always refrained from clamoring for protection. There is a great need for rationalization in this area, and in many cases it is likely to come via direct government action, rather than through more slowly working market forces. Argentina, Chile, and Peru have recently taken steps to rationalize their auto industry.[13] This could lead to frictions, but it must be borne in mind that some kind of rationalization in high cost, excessive capacity import substituting activities is quite desirable from the viewpoint of economic efficiency.

There is indeed the need to rethink in Latin America the whole traditional policy of protectionism. It is not only that it has yielded excessive protection; it has also lacked a clear set of objectives. Protectionism typically leads, at least in the short run, to inefficiency in the use of resources, as well as to income redistribution in favor of the protected entrepreneurs, at the expense of the rest of society. It is possible that "infant entrepreneurs" will eventually justify those subsidies by their "learning by doing." Notice that I put the emphasis on entrepreneurs, not on industries. If this is accepted, I see little to justify Latin American countries sudsidizing foreign entrepreneurs in protected industries, as those foreign entrepreneurs are hardly "infants" and, by definition, are in activities which cannot pay their own way without protection. Protected industries, if they are going to be encouraged at all, should then as a rule be reserved to national entrepreneurs to be, so to speak, their training ground, and in that way justify their social cost. The same would apply to special subsidies to protected industries via credit, tax rebates, etc. Ideally, effective tariffs, or the tariff-equivalence of other measures, should be gradually lowered even to infant entrepreneurs, but while they remain, say, above 20 percent for a given activity, that activity should be reserved to national entrepreneurs, unless very special circumstances or national objectives dictate otherwise.[14] Furthermore, national entrepreneurs who in the past have benefited from protection would not be allowed to sell out to foreign investors, unless they returned to the national treasury the accumulated difference between the effective protection they received and the 20 percent limit. But I suspect that the unpopularity of this proposal among foreign investors will be easily exceeded by the enthusiasm with which it will be rejected by Latin American protectionists.

Another illustration of the need for closer coordination between DFI and protectionist policies is found in bans of "luxury" imports leading to their domestic production by foreign firms. A rationale may be given for banning soft drink imports while allowing the establishment of a Coca-Cola plant within the country, but such a rationale is likely to be weak. (Even when they do not receive protection, one may doubt the usefulness to the host country of DFI whose major strength is a brand name for manufactured consumer goods whose worldwide fame has been created by persistent advertising.)

A rationalization of protectionist policy would also help to check another negative influence exerted by foreign business on Latin American economies, this time not through DFI but through meretricious peddling of capital goods. More than one Latin American white elephant has been conceived in unholy marriage between heavily protected local entrepreneurs, often managers of public enterprises, and unscrupulous foreign, very frequently European, suppliers of machinery and equipment.

The previous paragraphs should be enough to dispel the notion that because more and more of DFI is going to promote Latin American industrialization, in contrast to old-fashioned DFI in export-oriented natural resource exploitation, the need to control DFI has lessened. From a purely economic viewpoint, in fact, it may well be that the "old-fashioned" DFI provided greater benefits to host economies.

Latin American ability to generate domestic savings has outstripped capacity to produce indigenous technological advances, and even to apply knowledge available from the rest of the world. But it is strongly felt that this is no reason to neglect a close scrutiny of *royalty and patent agreements*, not all of which are deemed appropriate to bring in desired knowledge at least cost. Government revision of royalty agreements between Colombian and foreign firms is said to have successfully reduced outward payments without sacrificing the technological inflow over the last few years. The Colombian regulations on the licensing of technological transfers markedly influenced the relevant parts of the Andean foreign investment code. Now Argentina has also introduced comprehensive regulations in this field, adding the interesting twist of requiring that fees for technological transfers be based not on sales, but on the profits of Argentine firms.

These measures can be interpreted partly as attempts to improve host country bargaining power in areas where international markets are thin and imperfect, and where the knowledge of those markets on the part of individual Latin American firms is weak. Just the fact that the new regulations state that all patents, trademarks, and agreements for sale of technology will have to be registered and approved by the government, improves the negotiating position of local firms vis-à-vis foreign suppliers. I am told that many a Colombian firm has hinted to that country's committee on royalties its willingness to have proposed agreements rejected by the government, for the sake of a second bargaining round with foreign suppliers. Such committees also keep tabs on the costs to host countries of technological transfers from parents to subsidiaries, and can reject agreements which restrict the freedom of host country firms to export, or to buy foreign goods from the cheapest source. In other words, they also serve as a mild form of antitrust, combating clauses which act in restraint of free trade. Note that these measures go beyond trying to deal with distortions within the host country; they are meant to handle far from competitive world markets.[15]

Another obvious way in which Latin American countries can increase their bargaining power is by acting jointly in negotiations with foreign investors, so as to avoid self-defeating competition among themselves. Remember the history of corporate regulation within the United States, when the Massachusetts law was undercut by competition from "loose" New Jersey and Delaware, or note the pointless recent competition among states of the United States in their tax laws, which has eroded their tax base without much net effect on total investment.[16] These considerations provide the rationale behind the desire of countries forming the Andean Common Market to have common foreign investment guidelines. Just as such a market, in its early stages, calls for a common minimum external tariff, it makes sense for it to have some kind of common minimum code for DFI.

Behind the trends reviewed in this section, one can detect not only "growing nationalism," but also growing sophistication on the part of Latin American policy makers, even though the new regulations can sometimes substitute new irrationalities for old ones. Of all the "gaps" separating the developing from the developed, one of the widest has been the gap in knowledge and bargaining know-how when a host country sat to negotiate with a foreign investor (witness the negotiations between post-Sukarno Indonesia and foreign investors). For Latin America this gap is narrowing, and hopefully one will soon see in each country scores of officials trained in both foreign business schools and even in MNCs, who then put their experiences to work for their countries by negotiating new contracts with foreign investors. There is much Latin America can learn from a close study of the *modus operandi* of the MNCs, even where the development model being followed is one hostile to the philosophy of MNCs.

All of this implies that in the future no empty references to the "sanctity of contracts" should impede a flexible approach to recontracting and renegotiations, as new circumstances emerge in host countries and in the world economy. The concept of renegotiating contracts is hardly novel for the industrialized countries; note, for example, how the Pentagon frequently renegotiates with its contractors. Note also how scores of labor contracts as well as international commitments had to be put aside by the presidential announcement of August 15, 1971.

U.S. AND INTERNATIONAL REACTIONS TO LATIN AMERICAN POLICIES TOWARD DFI: MINIMIZING FRICTION

Latin American policies toward DFI, old and new, are very likely to remain the major source of friction between the United States and Latin America for the foreseeable future. There is no issue where differences in the intellectual and emotional climate, north and south, are more marked. With other foreign investors (such as Europeans and Japanese), with fewer investments, less historical deadweight, and more modest hemispheric political roles, the climate is better, although not exempt from tension. My colleague Benjamin Cohen tells me that South Koreans view U.S. investors very much in the same light as Latin Americans view the Japanese.

While friction is, in the nature of things, inevitable, it need not lead to apocalyptic results. Let us first look at some recent events and then conclude with some reflections on a few ideas which may avoid over the long run a replay, on a more massive scale, of the Cuban-U.S. hysterics of 1959-61.

A first thing to note is that U.S. policies in this area during 1969 and 1970 were quite reasonable, under the circumstances. One can cite the nonapplication of the Hickenlooper amendment in the IPC-Peruvian dispute and, going outside the region, the quiet diplomatic settlement of disputes between U.S. investors and Algeria. The "low profile" had a good chance of becoming a successful U.S. Latin American policy, in spite of misguided criticism of it as "do-nothing." Better steady "do-nothing" than the previous unstable mixture of warm rhetoric, some tied aid, and an occasional invasion.

Unfortunately, the "low profile" appears to be changing to an ugly, tough one. The symptoms have been:

1. Threats to use international and bilateral concessional aid as a weapon in disputes between U.S. business firms and Latin American governments. This goes beyond even the Hickenlooper amendment, which at least gave some "grace period" for settlement, and left multilateral organizations out of those disputes.
2. Denial of access to near-commercial credit, such as that

provided by EXIMBANK, to countries which were in the process of negotiating settlement with foreign investors. While that type of credit is not an inevitable component of international transactions in goods like commercial airplanes, it is sufficiently common to make the denial or postponement of a routine request come close to economic boycott.

3. After much talk of trade preferences, in fact granted in 1971 by Europe and Japan,[17] and in spite of substantial and steady U.S. trade surplus with Latin America,[18] new Latin American export drives were dealt a blow by the 10 percent import surcharge announced by President Nixon on August 15, 1971, the negative psychological impact of which is perhaps more important than the real incidence. It would indeed be ironic if after years of preaching the need for export promotion in Latin America by many people, including international and U.S. aid agencies, and just when the message is getting through, the major industrialized countries turn protectionist. Is it the fate of Latin America to be always out of step, turning away from the world market when it is booming, as during the postwar days, and toward it just when it turns protectionist? At any rate, Latin American export pessimists were given much ammunition by the August 15th announcement.

These are very disturbing symptoms, one could almost say provocations, which could unleash an unfortunate cycle of reprisals and counterreprisals, leaving both sides politically and economically worse off at the end, and destroying institutions and rules of the game within which mutual adjustments can occur.

Over the last few years several proposals have been put forth to smooth the tensions which exist between MNCs and host countries.[19] One hears how truly "multinational" U.S. corporations with foreign investments are becoming, and how this trend represents a great advance over narrow nationalisms. But if at every sign of friction with a host government those companies run to enlist the power of the U.S. government on their side of the fight, their claim to "multinationality" will be regarded, with good reason, as hollow. Private foreign investors cannot have it both ways for very long. In a way, this point reflects the very old mistrust of conservative economics of mixing up government with private enterprise in shady proportions, a mistrust which should apply to international as well as national businesses. It suggests that government intervention in this area, via institutions such as the Overseas Private Investment Corporation (OPIC), does either too little or too much. If the U.S. government judges that certain foreign investments do clearly involve the U.S. national interest, then the U.S. government should become an open and declared partner in the venture, and should take clear responsibility for every aspect of the contract. This is what the French government does, as I understand it, with French investment in oil. During the oil crisis of 1970-71, private oil MNCs took on a quasi-public role, and the U.S. lifted antitrust regulations so they could present a common front. Similar considerations could apply where DFI provides industrialized countries with access to raw materials deemed strategic, for which open and competitive markets may be impossible even to imagine. But for those foreign investments which do not involve the U.S. national interest unambiguously, then the U.S. government should leave risk-taking as well as profits fully to the private entrepreneur.

Even under such an "arm's length" relationship between government and the foreign investor, it is not unreasonable to expect that the U.S. government will not remain totally indifferent if the existing business of one of its citizens is systematically abused and plundered abroad. India, after all, shows concern over the treatment received by second- and third-generation Hindus in Africa, and Chile watches over her emigrants in neighboring Patagonia. But it is dangerous to use receptivity to fresh DFI as criteria to discriminate among countries in matters relating to trade and aid. There is nothing in the postwar multilateral rules of the game, as embodied in organizations such as the GATT, and IBRD, and the IMF, which encourages a close link between trade and investment preferences. Even within the common market made up of the fifty U.S. states, Puerto Rico, and the Virgin Islands, while there is free trade in goods and free movement of labor, there remains a considerable amount of state legislation which limits the operations of banks and other financial institutions. Similarly, the world community should be able to create an environment in which each sovereign country can trade internationally as much as it wants and can, while reserving its right to follow more restrictive policies regarding the capital account of its balance of payments. Furthermore, it does not make much sense for foreign investors to become all worked up about new restrictions over DFI which a Latin American country may impose, when it is known that similar practices are tolerated by foreign investors in countries like Yugoslavia, Rumania, Japan, and Sweden.

The 1971 international monetary crisis dramatized the fact that not even the Atlantic community is yet ready to become an "optimum currency area," within which capital flows would be as smooth as those between London and Manchester. Greater future reliance on more flexible exchange rates and/or tighter controls over the capital account of the balance of payments is likely among many industrialized countries. In this setting, it is particularly anachronistic to press LDCs for relaxation of their regulations over certain types of capital flows.

A key characteristic of DFI is that it puts together into an indivisible package capital, technology, management skills, information about foreign markets, etc. Economists know about the inefficiencies created by "tied sales," and anyone who believes in the benefits of free competitive markets should be able to support efforts to give LDCs more options by creating, probably at low real costs, alternative and separate markets for *each* of these elements.

In the first place, international private capital markets for LDC bonds should be expanded and strengthened, facilitating access to them by those countries wishing to rely less on concessional aid and DFI. The expansion of international capital markets during the 1960s, and the degree of economic maturity reached by many Latin American countries make this option a promising one for the 1970s. If Hungary can tap the Eurobond market, at least the seven largest Latin American countries should be able to do the same in growing amounts.

International organizations such as the IBRD, and IADB, and the IFC have done remarkably little in the field of technological transfer. They could step up their efforts to act as clearinghouses of information as to where LDCs could obtain technological inputs in the cheapest way, and not necessarily tied to capital transfers. The socialist countries could be brought in to participate more actively in those licensing markets.

International and regional organizations could also be more involved in backstopping for LDCs in their search for information when those countries are in the process of negotiating with foreign investors. Unfortunately, the practices of some of those organizations have in fact been perverse in the past. Using the excuse that international private capital was available, they have refused to lend for host country investments in certain sectors, such as oil. They have thus abstained from helping to diversify not only the sources of capital, but, more critically, the channels through which Latin America has access to modern technology and information about the state of particular world markets.

Professor Charles P. Kindleberger has called for a sort of GATT to regulate MNCs, as well as to serve as an international ombudsman, charged with preserving competition, avoiding inconsistent national regulations of MNCs, and resolving conflicts. If sponsored by the United Nations, such an institution could be most useful in avoiding many of the difficulties we have reviewed. The idea, incidentally, is far superior to similar ones which have been proposed, but which restrict participation to Western Hemisphere nations. It is also superior to proposals for a multilateral investment guarantee scheme operated collectively by all OECD members. Such a scheme comes close to providing a framework for an investors' cartel. Indeed, this is exactly the reason why the *Economist* of London recently advocated that plan.[20]

The ideas reviewed in these last paragraphs are meant for the long run and say little about thorny transitional disputes between

Latin American countries, foreign investors, and the United States. When viewed in the midst of battle, those disputes can be exasperating and dismaying, although exhilarating for those in search of confrontations. When one is gloomily contemplating such a panorama, it is comforting to review the record of French-Algerian relations. After a bloody war and many frictions and maneuvers, including going to the brink and trying to bring other parties into their dispute,[21] they seem to have worked out a civilized and mutually profitable arrangement. Surely the United States and Latin America can do even better. Indeed, the end of total U.S. hegemony in the hemisphere could open the way for a genuine improvement in U.S.–Latin American relations.

NOTES

AN EARLIER VERSION of this paper was presented at a conference on "Trade and Investment Policies in the Americas," held October 7-8, 1971, at Southern Methodist University. Comments from Benjamin I. Cohen and Richard N. Cooper are gratefully acknowledged.

1. See testimony of Stephen Hymer in pt. 4, "The Multinational Corporation and International Investment," *Hearings before the Subcommittee on Foreign Economic Policy of the Joint Economic Committee*, Congress of the United States (Washington: U.S. Government Printing Office, 1970), pp. 906-11.

2. Ragnar Nurkse, "International Investment Today in the Light of Nineteenth-Century Experience," reprinted in Richard N. Cooper, ed., *International Finance* (Baltimore: Penguin Books, 1969), p. 367.

3. Harry G. Johnson, "Theoretical Problems of the International Monetary System," also in Cooper, *International Finance*, p. 315.

4. *New York Times*, May 31, 1971.

5. Roberto Campos and Aldo Ferrer, "Inversión Extranjera y Desarrollo Económico Latinoamericano (Versión Preliminar)," mimeographed (Washington, D.C., December 26, 1967).

6. Laurence Birns and Robert H. Lounsbury, "The Art of Survival in Latin America," *Columbia Journal of World Business* 6, no. 4 (July-August 1971): 43.

7. Nelson A. Rockefeller, *The Rockefeller Report on the Americas: The Official Report of a U.S. Presidential Mission for the Western Hemisphere* (Chicago: Quadrangle Books, 1969), p. 17; *New York Times*, August 15, 1971.

8. For an interesting discussion of problems raised by intracorporate sales techniques, see Richard N. Cooper, *The Economics of Inter-Dependence: Economic Policy in the Atlantic Community* (New York: McGraw-Hill Book Co., 1968), pp. 101-5. Cooper suggests a test which perhaps can be applied to Latin America and U.S. data, and which consists of inquiring

whether for specific activities book profit rates are higher for parent firms with Latin American investments than for comparable firms without such investments.

9. *New York Times*, April 5, 1971.

10. See for example "The Ugly Japanese?" *Wall Street Journal*, May 12, 1971, and "A Foreign Legion Routs the French," *Business Week*, May 8, 1971. On the other hand, French publications become highly emotional on Algeria, but take an almost amused tone when dealing with U.S. DFI difficulties in Latin America, as does *The Economist* of London, which, however, loses its cool over Middle East oil, saying things like:

> Once upon a time, had a group of backward countries, with highly unstable governments and a reputation for persistent commercial bad faith, tried to hold the western economies to ransom as the oil producing governments of the Middle East are now doing, they would have seen the gunboats steaming up the Gulf in double-quick time (Editorial, January 30, 1971)

11. This discussion of joint ventures draws heavily on the work of Louis T. Wells, Jr. of the Harvard Business School. See in particular his unpublished paper "Effects of Policies Encouraging Foreign Joint Ventures in Developing Countries."

12. Eduardo Frei Montalva, "The Second Latin American Revolution," *Foreign Affairs* 50, n. 1 (October 1971): 89.

13. See "Car Output Laws in Argentina, Peru, Chile to Give Nations More Control of Industry," *Wall Street Journal*, June 10, 1971.

14. For more on this point, see Carlos F. Díaz-Alejandro, "Direct Foreign Investment in Latin America," in Charles P. Kindleberger, ed., *The International Corporation* (Cambridge: M.I.T. Press, 1970), especially pp. 325-29. The 20 percent limit is, of course, arbitrary; it is assumed that the real exchange rate in the host country is not too out of line with the "equilibrium" one.

15. See the impressive work of Constantine V. Vaitsos, "Transferencia de Recursos y Preservación de Rentas Monopolísticas," *Revista de Planeación y Desarrollo* 3, no. 2 (July 1971): 35-72.

16. See Richard N. Cooper, "National Economic Policy in an Interdependent World Economy," *Yale Law Journal*, 76, no. 7 (June 1967): 1293-97. The use by states and municipalities of their privilege to float tax-exempt securities for the purpose of raising funds for new businesses locating within their borders is another example of harmful competition among political units.

17. My colleague Richard N. Cooper, in a recent unpublished paper, argues that the EEC scheme for generalized tariff preferences will offer, in fact, very little additional incentive to exports of developing countries. But at least that scheme will consolidate LDC gains in the European market, in contrast with the threat of backsliding implicit in the U.S. measures.

18. For many years, Latin American complaints about a negative trade balance with the United States, and of its composition involving the exchange of unprocessed raw materials for manufactured goods, were rejected by U.S. officials with the (theoretically correct) observations that what matters is the *global* balance of payments and that there is nothing basically wrong with trading raw materials for manufactures. It is then mildly mind-

blowing to read that the United States has been using exactly the Latin American arguments regarding U.S. trade with Japan.

19. Within the Latin American context, see in particular Albert O. Hirschman, *How to Divest in Latin America, and Why*, Essays in International Finance no. 76 (Princeton, N.J.: Princeton University, November 1969), and Paul N. Rosenstein-Rodan, "Multinational Investment in the Framework of Latin American Integration," in *Multinational Investment in the Economic Development and Integration of Latin America* (Inter-American Development Bank, 1968). See also Charles P. Kindleberger, *American Business Abroad* (New Haven: Yale University Press, 1969), especially Lecture 6, and Raymond Vernon, *Sovereignty at Bay: The Multinational Spread of U.S. Enterprises* (New York: Basic Books, 1971).

20. The candid line of reasoning is as follows:

> The offending host government might always calculate that bygones will be bygones if it waits long enough. . . . To complicate matters, other countries may not have suffered at all from the defaults of a non-paying host government, and will be far quicker to forgive past misbehaviour, their companies would then enjoy a handsome advantage in that country if their guarantee schemes started giving cover there again. All of which points to the need for a multilateral investment guarantee scheme operated collectively by all OECD members, such as the World Bank is now chewing over.

The quotation is from an article entitled "From Gunboats to Insurance," *Economist*, November 6, 1971.

21. The specter of collusion among major industrialized countries became tangible during the most recent Algerian-French dispute, when it looked as if the United States gave in to French pressure and threatened to block U.S. imports of Algerian liquefied natural gas until Algeria settled with France. But fortunately for LDCs, differences of interests and rivalries among the rich appear stronger than their desire for a joint venture. This is reflected in the following excerpts from an editorial in the *Wall Street Journal*, June 18, 1971:

> High-handed treatment by producing countries of international oil companies is not something the United States would want to encourage. . . . Still, there are serious questions about whether the U.S. government should pass judgment on a dispute between Algeria and France. . . . The United States will badly need fuel in the years ahead.

JOSEPH GRUNWALD

Latin American Economic Integration And U.S. Policy

THE EMPHASIS in U.S. policy toward Latin America has shifted since the early 1950s from a preoccupation with military security and the cold war to consideration of economic and social matters. The tenor of the new policy, increasingly stressing developmental concerns, was first expressed through the Act of Bogotá in 1960, then through the Alliance for Progress subscribed to in Punta del Este in 1961, and again in Punta del Este in 1967 when the United States offered support to a Latin American common market. This change in policy emphasis "constitutes a shift from a concentration upon objectives of primary interest to the United States to those of primary concern to Latin America."[1]

Latin American reaction to U.S. policies has been ambivalent. While Latin American governments have almost always sought a special relationship with the United States, the dominant economic, political, and military power in the hemisphere since World War I, they have often shown hostility to the northern giant. Embraces and admiration of the United States and its ideals have alternated, or frequently existed simultaneously, with rejection and antagonism.

Whatever U.S. policy may be, it will always be found suspect by many Latin Americans, for the region is a conglomeration of nations and peoples governed by regimes representing a fraction of the population and often only tiny but powerful interest groups. While intellectuals are generally alienated from their governments, the great mass of the population has been, at least until recently, politically uninvolved and inert. Even if U.S. policy were oriented solely toward development and social change, there would be opposition by influential sectors favoring the status quo. As a mixture of developmental, military, and other considerations, U.S. policy may run counter to every conceivable prejudice in Latin America; certain segments of the intellectual community, for instance, may consider a laudable development component only a cover for the true motive of the United States—the political and economic domination of the region.

THE BILATERAL RELATIONSHIP

The United States has always considered its relationships and responsibilities toward Latin America special. Latin American countries have largely accepted this status, quarreling among themselves for U.S. favors and only rarely, until recently, banding together to countervail its power. The inter-American system established by the United States has promoted neither unity nor independence in Latin America. Following World War II the system—then embodied in the newly created Organization of American States (OAS)—served primarily as one of many regional security arrangements responding to the emergence of the Soviet Union as a leading world power.

At that time Latin American governments began to concentrate their energies on obtaining the maximum benefits from their special relationships with the United States, seeking with some success U.S. financial aid, capital investment, and technical assistance. As a consequence, commercial and financial ties within the hemisphere are now bilateral, between the United States and each Latin American nation. Development assistance, including aid from multilateral institutions such as the Inter-American Development Bank (IDB), goes for the most part to individual countries for their national programs, rather than to groups of countries for regional purposes. Neither the individual countries nor the aid-giving institutions have seriously worked to identify and promote regional investment projects.

On the contrary, Latin American representatives at inter-American meetings have been preoccupied with protecting their countries' sovereignty. Nonintervention from within the hemisphere has become as important to them as nonintervention from outside is to the United States. Though their fear is of the overwhelming presence of their northern neighbor, their persistent reaffirmation of national sovereignty has limited their relations with each other. Moreover, because all members of the inter-American system have been considered juridically equal and "to have an equal interest in the prosecution of all the agreed purposes of the system . . . the formation of blocs or subgroups on the basis of special interests" has been strongly opposed."[2] The enormous difference in economic and political power between the "colossus of the North" and Latin American countries has tended to make a true hemispheric partnership impossible.

THE LATIN AMERICAN INTEGRATION MOVEMENT

By the 1950s, strong political motivations for regional integration had begun to emerge. Very few Latin American leaders were ready to speak openly, but the feelings of many were echoed by Chile's President Eduardo Frei in 1964, when he urged that "the twenty poor and disunited [Latin American] nations [form] a powerful and progressive union which can deal with the United States as an equal."[3] Latin American countries have become aware that they would be more powerful in international councils if they spoke as a region, with one voice, rather than dealing individually with the outside world.

While their collective bargaining power is an important motive for regional union, economic considerations have become the main rationale for regional integration. When it became apparent that industrialization based on import substitution within each nation could neither continue indefinitely nor reduce the region's dependence on the outside world, a number of Latin American countries decided to attempt closer economic cooperation among themselves, independent of their individual relations with the United States and therefore outside the inter-American system. Integration efforts in Latin America have already been successful enough to produce the Latin American Free Trade Association (LAFTA), encompassing all of South America (except the Guianas) and Mexico, and the Central American Common Market (CACM), including all but one of the countries of Central America. Partly because the members of the latter group had attained and were existing at a much lower level of development and therefore had fewer vested interests to defend, partly because the area is smaller and the countries geographically closer together, partly because of a more favorable demand for their products within their market, and especially because the area received greater financial support from the United States, CACM has made more progress than LAFTA since the groups were established in 1960.

The movement toward integration in LAFTA slowed down significantly in the second half of the 1960s. Formation of the group, after decades of failure and frustration, had been an enormous achievement. Prior to the 1950s, Latin American economic integration was a very remote idea. The signing of the Montevideo Treaty in 1960—unexpected by many people—unleashed grandiose anticipations that were patently unrealistic. The exaggerated hopes of the early LAFTA years have been replaced by an equally exaggerated disillusionment with regional integration. The euphoria fed by the easy success of the first rounds of tariff negotiations has disappeared with the need to make hard decisions. Had early expectations been more realistic, the later disappointment would not have been so deep. Latin American policy-makers have yet to show whether they are willing or able to take the politically difficult steps that are needed to accelerate the advance toward a common market. An encouraging portent is the Andean Subregional Integration Agreement signed in 1969. If this venture prospers, the major countries on the outside cannot easily remain aloof from the integration movement.

THE ECONOMIC RATIONALE

Latin American economies, although far from stagnating, did not grow fast enough during the 1960s to alleviate the area's grave economic and social problems. Severe underemployment and unemployment, exacerbated by a rapid population increase, may turn into an unsustainable burden unless the region's economic development can be significantly accelerated. But the promise of the first years of the last decade—the Alliance for Progress and U.S. aid—has withered. Neomercantilist tendencies have emerged in developed countries to bolster traditional restraints against exports, actual and potential, from low-income countries.

Difficulties in increasing or even maintaining their rates of growth and industrialization have forced Latin American countries during the last decade to turn from inward-looking industrialization toward international trade as a vehicle for development. In focusing their attention once again on exports, Latin Americans are not contemplating a return to the international trade patterns that existed before World War II; they are concerned not only with exporting traditional primary commodities but increasingly with producing manufactures for sale abroad. This stems from a recognition that the slow growth of national markets limits the expansion of industry and that industrialization cannot be efficient unless it is based at least in part on production for export.

A NEW EXPORT ORIENTATION

Many countries of Latin America demonstrated in the 1960s that they could not sustain alone the rapid growth and high rates of industrialization they had reached during the 1940s and 1950s. The economic slowdown is often attributed to an overemphasis on development of the industrial sector, aided by high protective tariffs, primarily at the expense of agriculture and mining. Industrialization was able to provide the impetus for growth during the 1940s and 1950s because of particularly favorable conditions for commodity exports, foreign investment, and financial assistance. Growth possibilities now are diminishing because they depend on industrial production for small home markets, traditional exports, and foreign aid.

It has become clear that a less protective trade policy can help the stagnant Latin American economies develop more rapidly through more efficient resource allocation. But for Latin Americans a fundamentally important aim of industrialization is the political and economic independence provided by self-sufficiency in manufacturing.

Latin American economists agree that the way out of the current economic impasse is through new development strategies oriented toward the promotion of international trade. A return to an emphasis on exports, however, should not mean concentrating production once more on traditional commodities for export at the expense of manufactures. Specializing in primary goods production might maximize the region's welfare in the short run, although the poor prospects for expanding such production significantly and the import restrictions, domestic subsidies, and other means of protecting inefficient competition in the advanced industrial countries make even that dubious.[4] Comparative advantages in international trade can be altered by development policies that seek to increase a country's economic welfare over the long run. Not only is the volume of production important to the economy, but also the kinds of goods produced. Thus a country or region whose current comparative advantages do not favor industrialization may elect to incur the short-run costs for the long-run advantages of industrialization.

The main thrust of a long-run development policy is to enlarge markets for protected Latin American manufactured goods. Heavy and medium industry, with expanded markets, would realize the benefits of economies of large-scale production[5] and resources could be more efficiently allocated and used.

REGIONAL INTEGRATION

Latin American economic integration could transfer import-substituting industrialization from a national to a regional scale, but Latin American statesmen do not accept this as the ultimate objective of development. Integration is considered "the most important mechanism for stimulating the diversification of exports"[6] and a step in the direction of worldwide free trade:

> As a first stage, this competition should be primarily among the Latin American countries themselves. In a second stage these countries should gradually accept competition from outside as their industries become stronger through the operation of the Latin American Common Market.... In this way, Latin American countries could participate more and more in a truly worldwide movement of trade liberalization.[7]

An economically integrated Latin America thus could be viewed as a subsystem of the world economy. The purpose of such a subsystem would be to change the structure of comparative advantage within which Latin American foreign trade takes place. At present the region finds itself "trapped" by the international division of labor, exporting primary commodities and at best only processed raw materials and light manufactures, and importing the products of technologically more complex industries. Regional integration would permit Latin America to enter some of the dynamic sectors of manufacturing, as a move not toward regional self-sufficiency but toward less unequal partnership in the world trading community. Latin Americans are quite aware that the bulk of international trade takes place among the industrial countries of the world. They want to participate in this interchange with products of growth industries in which they do not now have a comparative advantage.

In a less developed region like Latin America, where the small size of national markets limits production, the possibilities of gains from economies of scale appear to be great. The larger markets created by a customs union should lead to lower manufacturing costs, higher rates of investment, and more efficient allocation of resources in the region. In addition, existing idle industrial capacity could be put to use to increase production. Indications are, therefore, that a Latin American common market would have a direct and important influence in accelerating economic growth in the region.

ECONOMIC EFFICIENCY AND THE DISTRIBUTION OF BENEFITS

Elimination of trade barriers might result in a polarization of economic development, with the more industrial countries attracting most of the investment and the least developed losing some of their infant industries in regional competition. Economies of scale, transportation costs, and external economies[8] would all work to distribute production in such a way that the optimum results for the region would not necessarily coincide with the optimum results for the individual nations. Thus while the region's prosperity increased, economic growth in the member countries might not be equalized.

Integration would produce benefits as well as costs for each member nation, and the difference between the two determines the net effect of integration on a country's welfare. The benefits arise from the employment of idle resources, increased industrialization, diversification of exports, and other structural changes, some of which fall under the heading of "modernization." The costs represent the higher regional prices paid for products formerly imported from the outside. If the benefits outweigh the costs, there will be a net gain. Smaller and weaker countries would tend to have a smaller net gain than the more industrial countries—perhaps even a net loss. They might not be able to attract more industry, possibly even less than they would have had they instituted national policies of import substitution; in addition, because they must import a greater share of consumer goods than their more advanced partners, they must bear a higher proportion of the costs of trade diversion.

Political reality demands that member countries of a customs union be assured that all will share in the benefits of economic integration and that none will be disadvantaged. Some economic efficiency will have to be sacrificed in the process of trading regional growth for a reasonable distribution of income among individual countries. Thus economic efficiency is not the sole objective of Latin American economic integration. Its aim is to achieve the highest output for the region consistent with a "balanced distribution" of economic development among the member countries; this would not necessarily result in maximum regional production.

U.S. POLICY

From the end of the last century, when the idea of Latin American economic cooperation emerged, to about 1960, when the idea began to be implemented, U.S. economic policy toward Latin America underwent remarkably few changes. The United States viewed Latin American countries as export economies dedicated to the sale of their natural resources overseas. The economic interest of the United States lay principally in promoting private investment and enterprise and serving the business interests of its citizens in the area. Even the great alterations in the economic environment and in Latin America's development needs during the 1930s did not change this posture. The United States continued to see the Latin American republics as simple agrarian countries and producers of raw materials for export even while Latin America turned toward industrialization.

Politically the United States has been guided by a sense of special responsibility toward Latin America. As the senior member of the inter-American system the United States has established a rule of dealing separately with each republic in pursuit of its interests. This bilateralism did not disappear even during periods of close hemispheric cooperation such as World War I, the Good Neighbor era, and the early years of the Alliance for Progress. Cooperation among Latin American countries could never prosper within the bilateral framework.

U.S. ATTITUDES

Economic integration for Latin America is a move toward both economic and political viability that demands the region's increasing independence from the United States and the rest of the world. Because this objective goes against the traditions of U.S. policy in the Western Hemisphere—although not necessarily against the long-term interests of the United States—the United States has been reluctant to accept the integration movement and its probable consequences.

Early U.S. attitudes toward Latin American economic cooperation were reflected in the government's recommendation at the end of the last century of a hemispheric customs union embracing both Latin America and the United States. Rising protectionism in the United States resulted in the quick abandonment of this idea for bilateral trade agreements between the United States and individual Latin American nations. In the 1950s the United States turned from a protectionist to a relatively free trade position. It continued to deal with Latin American countries bilaterally, strengthening these relations in the name of hemispheric security. Only in the late 1950s did the United States begin to accept Latin American integration efforts, as long as they conformed with the rules set for regional trade groupings by the General Agreement on Tariffs and Trade (GATT), which appeared to be concerned primarily with developed countries.

In the first four years of the Alliance for Progress (1961-65) U.S. thinking began to shift from the idea of hemispheric free trade and pure bilateralism to a concept of economic integration as a means of developing Latin America. Under the Alliance for Progress, U.S. assistance was made available to the Central American Common Market (CACM). But U.S. policy makers viewed economic cooperation among the larger economies of the region as a Latin American affair and avoided any direct relationship with the Latin American Free Trade Association (LAFTA) lest it be regarded as interventionism. Since 1966 a Latin Americanwide common market has had the formal support of the United States and U.S. officials have embraced the idea of a Latin American common market as an important vehicle for accelerating economic growth in the region.

A U.S. POLICY FOR INTEGRATION

Despite official endorsement of regional economic efforts, no effective change has been made in certain key aspects of U.S. policy. This is due partially to U.S. reluctance to interfere in an area that is held to be an exclusive Latin American concern. But the apparent decline in Latin American enthusiasm for significant sacrifice in support of common arrangements also encourages U.S. apathy. A decisive move by the United States to subordinate its bilateral relations with individual countries in favor of regionwide integration assistance programs might jeopardize those countries' friendship and create new problems in U.S.–Latin American relations. Such a shift in policy is the more difficult to support because of the uncertain prospects for Latin American economic integration. And there is still a lingering question whether a regional common market is compatible with the free trade policy that the United States has subscribed to since the Great Depression; moreover, there is still doubt whether regional support for Latin American development would be more productive than traditional bilateral aid.

A potential conflict with private economic interests in the United States may also restrain institution of a policy change. Some U.S. investors, like indigenous industrialists in the area, prefer to operate with a minimum of competition behind the protection of high national trade barriers rather than be exposed to the uncertainties of regional free trade. Furthermore, Latin American economic integration poses a threat to the traditional export markets of U.S. firms; in a highly protected area, imports would be replaced; in an efficiently integrated area without high tariff walls, imports might not be replaced but regional exports might become competitive. Protectionist sentiment in the United States and other developed countries has been stirred by Latin American production of goods other than traditional exports at competitive world market prices. Economic integration could further reduce production costs and increase the conflict between U.S. domestic producers' interests and Latin America's development needs.

But the basic reason for U.S. failure to reduce its bilateral ties in favor of regional relations is the lack either of any compelling need to do so or of any significant pressure from Latin American governments to change the bilateral system.

Thus inconsistencies from the past dominate current U.S. attitudes. While the United States supports an accelerated move toward a common market, it is deeply committed to, and conditioned by, its bilateral trade relations and aid programs in Latin America. Since the Korean War, aid has been the front-line instrument of U.S. policy in the region. It has been concerned with the progress of individual Latin American countries rather than with the advancement of the region as a whole. Both U.S. aid practices and other policies must change if Latin American integration is to become a serious objective of U.S. policy. The whole relationship between Latin American countries and the United States that has grown up over the last century must be modified.

BILATERAL VERSUS INTEGRATION ASSISTANCE

As an active supporter of Latin American integration, the United States must make a fundamental reappraisal of its aid policy. Assistance is currently geared to national development, each economy competing individually for U.S. aid. Not only has integration assistance to Latin America been very meager, but national bilateral aid has often worked against integration. In the past, financing has been provided for projects designed only for the national welfare of the recipient, without much regard for a larger, regional efficiency.

The most effective contribution the United States can make to Latin American development is aid for regional objectives rather than for national purposes.[9] A little over $30 million annually went to integration projects for all of Latin America during the six-year period 1961-66, according to AID and IDB data. Those projects, multinational in scope—such as international roads and integration industries—or devoted to regional export promotion, monetary arrangements, and training and research institutions, received less than 5 percent of "national aid" to the area for that period.

A U.S. program that continues bilateral aid at its present level cannot provide a significant impetus toward integration. It would offer no incentive to Latin American governments to move more boldly toward regional integration. As long as U.S. assistance continues to help Latin American countries individually, they may have more to gain from the United States through autarkically oriented development programs than through regional schemes whose risks the proposed U.S. integration assistance could not begin to cover.[10]

UNDERWRITING THE RISKS OF INTEGRATION

Because of the lack of homogeneity among LAFTA countries, they would probably not share equally in the benefits of economic union, and some might suffer welfare losses, at least temporarily. The less industrialized countries might have to divert their imports from low-cost outside manufacturers to higher cost Latin American producers.[11] Such countries might need balance-of-payment assistance during early stages of the integration process.

In many countries where inefficient industries have been built up behind high levels of protection, adjustment funds would be needed to provide loans to those suffering serious losses in the integration process. Funds might also be needed for retraining labor dislocated because of the formation of the common market. Labor retraining is recognized as "primarily a development measure"; aid to industries, on the other hand, must be selective if it is to be more than a palliative.[12]

THE CASE FOR U.S. AID FOR AN INTRAREGIONAL PAYMENTS UNION

An intraregional monetary arrangement offering temporary financial support to countries adversely affected by trade liberalization has long been considered an important element in Latin American economic integration. The specter of trading deficits deters many Latin American countries from joining wholeheartedly in the integration movement. Practically every LAFTA country fears that its products might not be sufficiently competitive with those of other countries in the bloc, and, therefore, that a speedy reduction in trade barriers might drastically increase its imports during the transition period without expanding its exports correspondingly. A system of intraregional cooperative financial arrangements to tide countries over regional deficits could remove a serious stumbling block on the road to a common market.[13]

It is doubtful whether an effective Latin American payments union could be established without a specific contribution by the United States. While a clearinghouse needs only small resources of its own and therefore can be established without any outside assistance, a more comprehensive scheme involving credits to ease temporary balance-of-payments disequilibria would need external financing if for no other reason than to get started. Of course, in order to make a union operate efficiently the member countries themselves would have to subscribe a part of their own reserves.

The United States in 1967 promised "a substantial contribution to a fund that will help ease the transition into an integrated regional economy."[14] The purpose of that adjustment or "buffer" fund was "to contribute to the solution of problems in connection with the balance of payments, industrial readjustments, and retraining of the labor force."[15] The U.S. commitment to provide balance-of-payments support could easily be translated into support for a Latin American payments arrangement. The benefits resulting from a relatively small commitment—the U.S. contribution to the European Payments Union did not exceed $350 million—could be very high.

ECONOMIC INTEGRATION AND INDEPENDENCE

Events in the European and, to a lesser extent, Central American common markets have recently reinforced Latin Americans' ambivalent attitudes toward integration. Many previous proponents of regional economic cooperation decided that a Latin American common market on the European model might be highly vulnerable to economic penetration by the United States. Experience showed that European integration was paralleled by the rapid expansion of giant U.S. international corporations; it appeared that U.S. subsidiaries had grown faster than European firms.[16] Suddenly some Latin American intellectuals have had second thoughts about integration, arriving at the same position of doubt as some business groups in the region, though mostly for different reasons.

The question has increasingly been raised in Latin America whether regional integration, born of a search for economic independence, might not lead to an even greater dependence on the United States. The first stage of the economic independence movement, in the forties and fifties, concentrated on strictly national, autarkically oriented industrialization. But it neither brought a sound and lasting acceleration of growth nor reduced economic dependence on the outside world.

There is a growing fear in Latin America that a regional effort now to permit more efficient and advanced development and vigorous industrialization might result in even greater foreign dominance. The new industrialization would be much more complex and sophisticated and would require more external capital and expertise. Thus the vision of a strong Latin America made independent and powerful by economic union is disturbed by the nightmare of a "hegemony of U.S. macro-enterprises . . . that could eventually relegate Latin America to the status of a minor appendage of the United States."[17] Foreign economic penetration has been increasingly controlled under recent national policies, but many Latin Americans believe that with the progress of economic integration national control over foreign enterprise would not be replaced by an adequate regional foreign investment policy. These fears are compounded by the knowledge that the United States has been a champion of freedom for foreign investors.

The shift in the middle of the 1960s in U.S. policy in favor of a Latin American common market nourished the new doubts. U.S. expressions of support culminated in the meeting at Punta del Este, Uruguay, in April, 1967, when the heads of the states of the inter-American system subscribed to a program for gradually establishing a common market. Latin Americans, looking at the past relationship of the United States with the region and the U.S. coolness to a Latin American common market before the 1960s, have become suspicious of this sudden interest in their integration movement.

INTEGRATION AND TRADE PREFERENCES

In trying to implement a mixture of an inward- and outward-oriented strategy, Latin Americans have found an inhospitable climate in the world around them. Trade prospects for traditional products are not encouraging, trade blocs restraining imports have emerged, trade barriers in developed countries discriminate against goods from the region, and no financial or other commercial incentives are offered for their exports. To overcome these obstacles Latin American countries have concentrated their efforts not so much on integration as on improving the conditions of world trade in primary products and on obtaining preferential access to developed-country markets for their industrial commodities.

The goal of trade preferences and of a Latin American common market is to foster industrialization. It is not clear, however, whether the methods are entirely compatible. Preferences for manufactured goods could well delay the development of a common infrastructure for the Latin American countries, which is considered an important objective of the integration process. They could weaken the need for tariff reduction among Latin American countries, perpetuating the small intraregional trade in manufactures and allowing parallel national industrialization policies with all of their inefficiencies to continue.[18]

Nevertheless, trade preferences in developed-country markets, together with regional integration, are likely to accelerate Latin American industrialization more than would either of the two measures alone. While preferences would increase access for the region's manufactures to extra-regional markets, an external tariff around a regional common market would give the same commodities a relative price advantage in Latin American markets. The two policies would reinforce each other's positive effects on investments and therefore on economic growth. For some investors in the Latin American area, trade preferences in developed-country markets would provide the main stimulus for industrial expansion; for others, the principal incentive for investment would come from a Latin American common market.

The magnitude of trade preferences could be made contingent on the degree of intraregional trade liberalization, so that the greater the tariff reductions among Latin American countries, the greater those granted in the U.S. market. Preferences could be keyed to the countries' degree of industrial development. For example, the big three—Argentina, Brazil, and Mexico, which at present have the most to gain from developed-country trade preferences for manufactured goods—might be required to reduce intraregional tariffs to a greater extent than the other Latin American countries to receive the same level of tariff concessions; or favored treatment might be offered the least developed countries in the region—Bolivia, Ecuador, Paraguay, and the Central American republics. In this manner trade preferences would constitute an incentive for trade liberalization and so stimulate the integration process.[19] In view of the fact that trade preferences are nonreciprocal—there is no direct *quid pro quo* for the developed countries—it would be difficult to argue that the tying to integration constitutes intervention.

Just as the European countries in a drive to regain their self-confidence clamored for "trade not aid" after the first few years of the Marshall Plan, so now Latin Americans tend to emphasize more favorable trade conditions from the developed countries (particularly since U.S. foreign aid is declining). A general improvement in world trade conditions might help to foster integration possibilities in Latin America, as was the case in Europe during the 1950s. Integration while Latin America's international trade is stagnating would be politically difficult if not impossible.

CHANGES NEEDED

Further steps toward Latin American integration would be in the best interest of the United States. Although the United States can hardly be blamed for the difficulties encountered in the economic integration effort since 1960, its bilateral relations with individual Latin American governments have impeded regional integration efforts. Despite its acknowledgment that regional integration may contribute substantially to increasing growth rates in Latin America, the United States has offered only verbal support for LAFTA since its inception. (In Central America it has moved from verbal to active support and has become an important factor in the region's progress toward a common market.)

The United States is in a position to facilitate the difficult transition from the current malfunctioning integration machinery to a Latin American common market. Its success in doing so will depend not only on its specific policy measures but also on a broad understanding of its economic relations with the region. The regional integration process for a group of developing countries must be seen as different from that of advanced economies.

The United States should reappraise and revise its aid policy in Latin America, increasing its aid for integration purposes even if this means sacrificing most aid to individual countries. If integration aid is small in relation to bilateral aid, it cannot stimulate progress toward Latin American economic union. Latin America needs external assistance to provide safeguards against potential losses from integration and to offer possibilities of immediate benefits for the least developed countries of the region; aid for integration would have to be geared to the general objective of assuring gains to all participants in a common market.

The success of new aid policies would depend not only on the amount of integration-supporting aid, but also on the commitment of continuing aid for the entire period of transition toward a regional common market, such aid to be administered by institutions in which Latin Americans would have a strong voice.

The public U.S. resources available for foreign aid have been sharply cut, and any massive expansion in the aid to low-income countries in general, and to Latin America in particular, is unlikely in the foreseeable future. The vital concern of U.S. policy makers should therefore be to get maximum productivity out of the small amount of aid funds available. Reducing bilateral assistance and concentrating aid for regional integration purposes could do this.

The U.S. bilateral aid program for Latin America at the beginning of the 1970s was about half the 1960-67 average, and the real resource flow was less than half the official average. No substantial results can be obtained from bilateral aid even if it is concentrated in only a few countries of the region. Little would be lost by giving up the present system, but much could be gained by rationalizing it and focusing it on regional integration.

Immediately after the institution of new U.S. policy, the region may not be prepared to take full advantage of integration aid. But when Latin American governments realize that the days of bilateral aid and special relationships with Washington are gone, they may be induced to adjust existing mechanisms and create new ones equipped to absorb integration aid efficiently.

Some larger Latin American countries would prefer to expand exports through developed-country concessions rather than through economic union with other Latin American countries. If the choice must be between extra- and intra-regional concessions, economic union would probably provide more long-run gains for Latin America than would selected, nonreciprocal tariff reductions by the developed countries. A combination of the two would, however, reinforce the positive effects of each on the economic growth of Latin America. The high-income countries could lower their tariffs on the goods of those developing countries that reduced trade barriers among themselves. Such a policy would be in line with the long-run objectives of trade liberalization and would stimulate less developed countries and regions to move in that direction in a world threatened by rising protectionist sentiment.

CONCLUSION

Two questions might be asked about external aid: Why should the United States now concentrate on assisting a Latin American effort in which important Latin American countries seem to have lost interest during the last few years? And, would not this change in U.S. aid policy signify intervention on the part of the United States in the internal affairs of the region?

During the late 1960s Latin American concerns appear to have shifted from regional economic cooperation to extraregional trade. But nothing happened during that period to make regional integration a less urgent matter than it was before. The economic viability of many Latin American nations is still highly questionable. And for all of them the prospects for rapid economic expansion are still circumscribed by their overall export possibilities. Regional integration offers the best immediate hope for Latin American countries to put their economic development on a sounder footing by permitting them to open themselves gradually to international trade without sacrificing their infant industries.

Appearances to the contrary, Latin American interest in regional integration is not dead. While little concrete progress toward a common market was made in the late 1960s, the movement toward cooperation is continuing. Even the big three—Argentina, Brazil, and Mexico, who seem to have been sitting on the sidelines—have joined all other Latin American countries in forming CECLA, the Special Coordinating Commission for Latin America, which in 1969 produced the Consensus of Viña Del Mar.

A shift in U.S. aid policy could indeed be regarded by Latin Americans as intervention. But the United States looms so large in the continent that any U.S. policy, whether of action or inaction, can be broadly conceived of as "intervention" and will certainly affect the course of Latin American events. The bilateral U.S. aid program has signified indirect interference in the domestic policies of the recipient countries; because the political nature of bilateral aid cannot be eliminated, such aid has often boomeranged. On the other hand, integration assistance can avoid most of the sensitive areas of internal national policies, so that the opportunities for outside interference are less.

Above all, U.S. policy in favor of Latin American integration should be expressed only in terms of offers of assistance that can be taken up or rejected by Latin Americans. No political or economic pressures, apart from aid offers, should force the region in the direction of a common market.

U.S. assistance for integration may strengthen the integration forces in Latin America. While at present there may not be any large groups in the region with strong commitments to further economic union, significant foreign support for integration purposes only is likely to stimulate greater local support for regional projects and economic cooperation, particularly if aid is oriented to reducing the risks of and compensating the losses from integration. Such incentives should make the potential benefits from integration much more visible to private and public local investors, thus, it is to be hoped, promoting interest groups with a stake in greater regional economic cooperation.

The renewed concern in Latin America for its independence from the outside world can perhaps best be relieved by regional economic integration. Latin American nations must choose whether to make some sacrifices for more serious regional cooperation or, following the line of least resistance, to continue the autarkic policies that limit their development and deepen their dependence on developed countries.

Integration support may help create not only an economically stronger but also a socially and politically more viable Latin America, one better equipped to assume the responsibilities and reap the benefits of an effective development policy. In giving this support, the United States would be showing statesmanship at its best, helping to shape an international environment conducive to peaceful economic and social evolution rather than, as it has so often in the past, reacting to crises that could have been avoided.

NOTES

1. John C. Dreier, "New Wine and Old Bottles: The Changing Inter-American System," *International Organization* 22 (Spring 1968): 490.
2. Ibid., p. 492.
3. Quoted in Robert N. Burr, *Our Troubled Hemisphere: Perspectives on United States-Latin American Relations* (Washington, D.C.: Brookings Institution, 1967), p. 87.
4. See Joseph Grunwald and Philip Musgrove, *Natural Resources in the Economic Development of Latin America* (Baltimore: Johns Hopkins Press for Resources for the Future, 1970), pt. 1, chap. 2, and pt. 2, the commodity chapters.
5. Unit costs of production decrease because of utilization of idle machinery and equipment or the introduction of new machinery and equipment, mass production techniques, and other technological improvements occasioned by a wider market. Economies of scale tend to be large in heavy industries and mass-production industries.
6. Carlos Sanz de Santamaría, in *Journal of Commerce*, April 14, 1967.
7. Raúl Prebisch, in ibid.
8. "External economies" are cost reductions to the firm which are due to factors external to the firm. For instance, locating an industry where other industries have already been operating will give it the advantages of a skilled labor pool, service industries, expert management, and perhaps cheaper raw materials, energy, and other inputs.
9. Not only should aid be given to multinational or regional groups, but it should be channeled through multinational institutions.
10. A case in point is the Latin American chemical fertilizer community that President Johnson proposed in 1965. The magnitude of the assistance anticipated—a concrete offer was never made public by the United States—was apparently not sufficient to overcome the obstacles perceived by Latin American countries. Moreover, the United States at almost the same time (1966) supported a strictly national fertilizer plant of questionable efficiency for Brazil, which weakened the idea of a regionwide fertilizer community.
11. Some less developed countries might consider lowered rates of industrialization a greater threat of integration than the loss of real resources.
12. Paul N. Rosenstein-Rodán, "Multinational Investment in the Framework of Latin American Integration," in Inter-American Development Bank, *Multinational Investment in the Economic Development and Integration of Latin America*, Round Table (IDB [1968]), p. 44.
13. "When countries commit themselves to liberalize trade and payments within the region, they are implicitly or explicitly reducing the options open to them to cope with their balance-of-payments difficulties." Anthony M. Solomon, "The Economic Integration of Latin America," *Department of State Bulletin* 57 (Oct. 23, 1967): 538.
14. President Johnson's speech at the inter-American summit meeting in Punta del Este on April 13, 1967, *Weekly Compilation of Presidential Documents* 3 (1967): 637.

15. *Declaration of the Presidents of America*, Punta del Este, April 1967, reproduced by the Organization of American States, p. 10.

16. Jean-Jacques Servan-Schreiber's *Le Défi Américain* (Paris: Editions Denoël, 1967), which analyzes the role of U.S. enterprise in Europe, allegedly sold more copies in Brazil than in France. Published in the United States as *The American Challenge*, trans. Ronald Steel (New York: Atheneum Publishers, 1968).

17. Marcos Kaplan, "Porqué no funciona la A.L.A.L.C.," *Mundo Nuevo*, 29 (Buenos Aires and Paris, November 1968): 8; authors' translation.

18. Manufactured goods have constituted an increasing proportion of intra-Latin American trade; they still account for only about 30 percent of the total; see Donald W. Baerresen, Martin Carnoy, and Joseph Grunwald, *Latin American Trade Patterns* (Washington, D.C.: Brookings Institution, 1965), p. 313, for 1959-63 figures. Intraregional exports constituted slightly more than 10 percent of Latin American exports to all countries in 1967; thus intra-area manufactured exports were not much more than 3 percent of total regional exports. Latin American manufactured exports to Latin America equal approximately 80 percent of those to the United States, and one-quarter of those to all countries.

19. Although such a scheme would be most feasible between the United States and Latin America, it could be worldwide: developed countries would grant trade preferences to those developing countries that reduce trade barriers to other developing countries.

DANIEL M. SCHYDLOWSKY

International Trade Policy In the Economic Growth of Latin America

THE SETTING

Perusal of official documents and conversations with policy makers reveal quite clearly the main goals of Latin American economic development policy. Latin American nations want a rapid increase in per capita income, the disappearance of unemployment, an increase in the equity of the distribution of income and wealth, price stability, and an absence of balance of payments problems. While there is considerable agreement on this list, important differences in emphasis exist among Latin American countries; some emphasize both price stability and lack of balance of payments problems, whereas others emphasize equity and employment. In the terms of the economist's jargon, the arguments of the utility function are the same, but the relative weights attached to these arguments vary from country to country.

The attainment of these goals in the postwar period has proved to be surprisingly difficult. Most countries have achieved a respectable rate of per capita growth; but despite very valiant struggles indeed, many countries still have very high rates of inflation. Almost all have recurrent balance of payments crises, all have a rate of unemployment considerably above what they regard as acceptable, and almost none have a high degree of equity in distribution.

The particular features of the situation, such as high rates of inflation with unemployment and unutilized installed capacity, tight money leading to even greater inflation, devaluations nullifying themselves through almost instantaneous price increases, etc., have puzzled both technical and nontechnical observers and added no little fuel to debates between conflicting and contradictory "explanatory theories." Thus monetarists and structuralists, protectionists and free traders have debated each other for years in the attempt to influence policy decisively and permanently. Yet after twenty-five years of postwar development, a consensus is not yet in sight. The same conflicting theories are still used to explain the Latin American economic situation and any one of them still fits only some of the facts. Nonetheless, most Latin American policy makers are belivers in one or another of these "partially true" faiths, and as a result they view reality through prisms which introduce distortions of varying magnitude. Consequently, the policies that are adopted are biased in a manner that often tends to aggravate the problems they are intended to deal with. Thus economic policy formulation in Latin America requires not only a more accurate theoretical framework but also the abandonment by policy-makers of outdated and only partially correct theoretical schema and their replacement by more appropriate eclectic views.

THE LATIN AMERICAN POLICY CONUNDRUM

A few basic and interrelated features of Latin American economic development explain in very large measure the mix of growth, balance of payments, and employment problems that Latin American countries have faced in the postwar period and continue to face today.

In simplest terms, the heart of the policy conundrum lies in the role and nature of Latin American industrial development. The industrial sector was chosen early in the postwar period as the motor of growth, employment, and better distribution. Policies of various sorts, most involving protection and tax exemptions, were designed to aid and intensify industry's rate of growth.

These policies were successful in the sense that industry has indeed been the leading sector in Latin American growth, with a growth rate consistently above that of GNP, as can be seen from Table 1. At the same time, however, industry in Latin America has been almost everywhere a foreign exchange using activity in the sense of requiring some imported inputs into the production process. As a result, as industrial growth proceeded, the import bill required to maintain industrial output grew. On the other hand, foreign exchange producing sectors have typically been the primary ones whose growth rate was in most cases below that of industry.[3] In consequence, the increase in demand for foreign exchange arising out of fast industrial growth rapidly put pressure on the slower growing supplies of foreign exchange from primary activities. These inherently different rates of

TABLE 1

THE GROWTH OF DOMESTIC PRODUCT AND OF MANUFACTURING IN SELECTED LATIN AMERICAN COUNTRIES
1950-52 to 1964-66

COUNTRY	GDP	MANUFACTURING GDP
Argentina	3.2%	4.4%
Brazil	5.3	7.8
Chile	4.0	5.0
Colombia	4.6	6.4
Dominican Republic	5.1	5.9
Guatemala	4.8	6.3
Honduras	3.6	6.8
Jamaica	7.4	8.1
Mexico	6.1	7.6
Nicaragua	5.8	7.5
Panama	6.4	9.8
Paraguay	3.1	2.6
Uruguay	1.5	2.5
Venezuela	6.4	9.3

SOURCE: OECD, National Accounts of Less Developed Countries.

growth would have imposed an early slowdown in industry's rate of growth, had it not been possible to free foreign exchange from existing uses through import substitution in industry. Such import substitution behind ever increasing protective barriers managed for some time to bring into balance the disparate rate of growth of production and use of foreign exchange. Table 2 shows this process at work in Brazil and Chile.

In the early seventies, the process of import substitution is virtually exhausted for the large Latin American economies and will very soon be for the medium and small ones. At this point a continued high rate of growth of industry is possible only if (a) increased foreign exchange is forthcoming for the primary industries, (b) new sources and ways of import substituting are devised, or (c) industry becomes a foreign exchange generator, not only a foreign exchange user. It is tempting to add foreign aid and foreign private investment to this list of options; however, this would not be strictly correct. Foreign aid by itself is likely to delay the reduction in the industrial rate of growth for some time; for repayment to take place, a very large contraction of industrial activity would be required to free the foreign exchange from other uses. Only if the public foreign debt arising from aid were to increase continuously at a compound rate of growth—a situation unlikely to be tolerated by either aid givers or aid receivers—could repayment be postponed forever. Foreign private investment is on balance only slightly more helpful. If it is in new industrial products, it will be foreign exchange using; indeed, it is likely to be even more import intensive than most existing industry.[4] Only if foreign private investment directs itself to the export-oriented industries will it contribute in some measure to alleviation of the conundrum.

The employment problem is also connected very closely to industrial development. In the early postwar period, industry was chosen as a leading sector in part because of the promise it seemed to hold of solving the unemployment problem then existing. Examination of the current situation shows that such hopes were not fulfilled. Instead, there is now considerable disillusion-

TABLE 2
THE DECLINING SHARE OF IMPORTS IN TOTAL SUPPLY

BRAZIL
1949-1964

IMPORTS AS PERCENTAGE OF TOTAL SUPPLY OF MANUFACTURED PRODUCTS BY USE

	1949	*1955*	*1959*	*1964*
Consumer goods				
Durable	60.1	10.0	6.3	1.6
Non-durable	3.7	2.2	1.1	1.2
Producer goods				
Intermediate	25.9	17.9	11.7	6.6
Capital	59.0	43.2	34.5	9.8
All manufactures	19.0	11.1	9.7	4.2

CHILE
1914-15 to 1963-64

SHARE OF IMPORTS IN DOMESTIC SUPPLY

	1914-15	*1927*	*1937-38*	*1952-53*	*1963-64*
Food, beverages, and tobacco	22.5	11.4	7.2	11.6	12.2
Textiles, clothing, and shoes	57.6	50.3	35.5	6.1	6.6
Wood products	23.2	4.9	3.2	1.5	2.0
Paper and printed matter	40.0	42.0	23.9	29.6	13.9
Leather and rubber products	24.6	36.5	16.3	31.1	17.3
Chemical products	91.3	71.3	60.6	51.8	38.5
Nonmetallic products	81.0	75.5	29.5	14.3	11.1
Metallic products	87.0	85.0	71.1	53.3	46.9
Total	51.5	43.8	29.9	26.0	24.6

SOURCES: Brazil: Joel Bergsman and Pedro S. Malan, "The Structure of Protection in Brazil," in B. Balassa et al., *The Structure of Protection in Developing Countries* (Baltimore: Johns Hopkins Press, 1971), Table 6.1. Chile: O. Munoz, "Long-run Trends in the Manufacturing Industry in Chile since 1914," as quoted in T. Jeanneret, "The Structure of Protection in Chile," in Balassa et al., Table 7.4.

ment with industry's potential for providing employment.[5] Explanations for the lack of success in this regard focus mostly on the relative prices of capital and labor, it being argued that capital goods have been too cheap and labor too dear to produce an adequate factor mix to lead to full employment. Such an analysis, while a natural outgrowth of the economic theory of factor use, leaves out a very important element, namely that installed capital is itself also substantially underemployed in Latin America. Thus unemployed labor coexists with unemployed capital and there is a quasi-Keynesian situation.[6] With capital utilized on the average at approximately one shift per day rather than the technical maximum of three, it would appear that the employment-giving potential of industry has been utilized to approximately a third of its real potential. It should be borne in mind, however, that the low degree of capital utilization has resulted from private decision-making which can be presumed to derive from profit maximization and is therefore "rational" in the economist's sense. At the same time, it does seem to be clear that from a public policy point of view this outcome is not the most desirable. Therefore, it becomes imperative to investigate the factors that cause such a divergence between the private profits and the public good.

THE FOREIGN EXCHANGE USING NATURE OF INDUSTRY

It is important to realize that the foreign exchange using nature of industry is not an immutable fact of life, but very substantially the result of the particular industrialization policy adopted by Latin American countries. The growth of industry was fostered by a set of import restrictions which cumulated over time and eventually led Latin American countries to have an exchange rate structure which is systematically biased against industrial exports and makes them unprofitable. Whereas the usual discussion focuses on *the* exchange rate, the amount of units of local currency which must be given up to obtain one dollar for purposes of financial transactions is best called the financial exchange rate. From the point of view of its impact on the economy, however, the financial exchange rate must be analyzed together with the trade taxation and other trade restrictions in force. Indeed, it is useful to think of an "exchange rate system" composed of the financial exchange rate and a large number of "commodity exchange rates" which are the multiple exchange rate equivalents of the existing taxes and other restrictions on commodity trade. Each commodity rate is defined as the number of units of domestic currency for which a dollar's worth of imports at CIF prices (or exports at FOB prices) of each particular commodity sells on the internal market. Each commodity rate is equal to the financial rate plus all the trade taxation and restrictions assessed on the import or export of that particular commodity. In general, there will be as many commodity rates as the economy has commodities tradeable internationally and often a single commodity may have more than one rate.[7]

In Latin America, most countries operate with a set of import restrictions which raise the commodity exchange rates for imports substantially above the financial rate. On the export side, some countries have operated at times with an export tax on traditional export commodities which has reduced the commodity exchange rate for traditional exports below the financial exchange rate. For example, Argentina was operating in 1966 with approximately the following exchange rate system:[8]

RATE	COMPOSITION		PESOS PER DOLLAR
Agricultural export	= Financial less 10% tax	=	200
Financial	= Financial	=	220
Non-traditional export	= Financial+18% tax rebate	=	260
Raw material import	= Financial+50% duties	=	330
Semi-manufactures import	= Financial+120% duty	=	460
Components import	= Financial+175% duty	=	600
Finished products import	= Financial+220% duty	=	700

A quick inspection of this rate structure will show why industry fails to generate foreign exchange. Industry buys its raw materials at an exchange rate of 330 pesos per dollar, its imported semimanufactures at 460 and its components at 600. This implies an average cost exchange rate for imported inputs of approximately 400 pesos per dollar. Domestic inputs have implicit exchange rates only slightly lower, since most domestic producers do not sell at prices much below those of similar imports. Industry's cost exchange rate for all material inputs is roughly between 380 and 420 pesos per dollar. At the same time, the wage rate industry pays reflects the average industrial exchange rate of about 600 pesos per dollar.[9] Hence total industrial costs are based on an exchange rate averaging 450 to 500 pesos per dollar. But a dollar's worth of exports yields only 260 pesos per dollar. Consequently, the would-be industrial export producer faces an implicit tax levied through the exchange rate system of close to 50 percent. The implications of this situation for the profit rate are rather dramatic.

TABLE 3

IMPORT COMMODITY RATES IN SELECTED LATIN AMERICAN COUNTRIES
(FINANCIAL RATE=1.00)

	BRAZIL 1967	CHILE 1961	MEXICO 1960
Nonmetalic mineral products	1.40	2.39	.96
Metallurgy	1.34	1.66	1.30
Machinery	1.34	1.84	1.30
Electrical equipment	1.57	2.05	1.25
Transport equipment	1.57	1.84	1.26-1.52
Wood products	1.23	1.35	1.14
Furniture	1.68	2.29	—
Paper and paper products	1.48	1.55	1.35
Rubber products	1.78	2.02	1.33
Leather products	1.66	2.61	1.20
Chemicals	1.34	1.94	1.24
Pharmaceuticals	1.37	—	1.12
Perfumes and soaps	1.94	—	1.10-1.22
Plastics	1.48	1.50	—
Textiles	1.81	2.82	1.30
Clothing	2.03	3.55	1.10
Food products	1.27	1.82	1.18
Beverages	1.83	2.22	1.28
Tobacco	1.78	2.06	1.31
Printing and publishing	1.59	1.72	1.13
Metal products	—	1.59	1.31
Fertilizers and insecticides	—	—	1.09

SOURCE: J. Bergsman and Pedro S. Malan, "The Structure of Protection in Brazil," Table 6.6, col. 5; T. Jeanneret, "The Structure of Protection in Chile," Table 7.8, col. 1; G. Bueno, "The Structure of Protection in Mexico," Table 8.7, col. 3; in B. Balassa, et al., *The Structure of Protection in Developing Countries*, (Baltimore: Johns Hopkins Press, 1971).

The Argentinian exchange rate structure is typical for Latin America, as can be seen from Table 3 which tabulates the im-

TABLE 4

THE ANTIEXPORT BIAS OF THE EXCHANGE RATE SYSTEM IN SELECTED LATIN AMERICAN COUNTRIES

PERCENTAGE OF ACTUAL FACTOR REMUNERATION PAYABLE ON THE BASIS OF EXPORT SALES

INDUSTRY	BRAZIL 1967	CHILE 1961	MEXICO 1960
Nonmetallic mineral products	.64	NVA	1.06
Metallurgy	.68	NVA	.49
Machinery	.71	.03	.57
Electrical equipment	.36	.11	.71
Transport equipment	.46	.15	.57*
Wood products	.78	.30	.75
Furniture	.32	NVA	—
Paper and products	.54	.21	.38
Rubber products	.41	NVA	.53
Leather products	.43	NVA	.61
Chemicals	.66	NVA	.5
Pharmaceuticals	.66	—	.65
Perfumes and soaps	NVA	—	.56-.77
Plastics	.49	.34	—
Textiles	.68	NVA	.79†
Clothing	.34	NVA	.83
Food products	.66	NVA	.59
Beverages	.14	NVA	.55
Tobacco	.40	.04	.53
Printing and publishing	.52	.31	.77
Metal products	—	.28	.48
Fertilizers and insecticides	—	—	.77

SOURCES: J. Bergsman and Pedro S. Malan, "The Structure of Protection in Brazil," Table 6.6; T. Jeanneret, "The Structure of Protection in Chile," Table 7.8; and G. Bueno, "The Structure of Protection in Mexico," Table 8.7, in B. Balassa et al., *The Structure of Protection in Developing Countries* (Baltimore: Johns Hopkins Press, 1971).

NOTE: NVA-negative value added; i.e., the cost of inputs exceeds the receipts from exports, hence no payments to factors are feasible.

* Railroad equipment only; motor vehicles have NVA.

† Cotton textiles.

port commodity rates by sector for Brazil, Chile, and Mexico. In turn, Table 4 presents for each industry in these three countries the factor remunerations payable on the basis of export business as a proportion of remunerations currently being paid on the basis of sales to the domestic market. A ratio of .6 means that export sales would only allow payment of 60 percent of the current wages, salaries, interest, profit, etc. By the same token, a ratio of .6 signifies that export sales can go forward only if the industry concerned has (marginal) costs of, or can cut costs to, 60 percent of current factor payments.

An additional and very important effect of the exchange rate structure is what may be called the "inefficiency illusion" of Latin American industry. It is generally "known" that Latin American industry is inefficient and uncompetitive. This "fact" is easily demonstrated by translating domestic industrial costs into dollars, which turn out to be substantially above the price of comparative imports. This computation uses the financial exchange rate. Since we know that domestic costs are based on the commodity exchange rates, which are usually considerably above the financial exchange rate, it is not surprising to find that domestic costs will be higher than international prices when converted at an exchange rate lower than the one on which they are based. This phenomenon, in the absence of the obvious explanation, has produced the inefficiency illusion effect and given Latin American governments and public the impression that they have an industrial structure totally out of kilter and hopelessly inefficient. The fact of the matter is, however, that much of the inefficiency is merely the result of an improper comparison using an exchange rate that is not applicable to the respective costs. When domestic costs are deflated by an appropriate exchange rate, i.e., one that is related to the commodity exchange rates, it turns out that Latin American industry is substantially more efficient than generally believed. Table 5 gives an indication of the size of the inefficiency illusion in Brazil by converting domestic production costs into dollars with an exchange rate reflecting the average cost rate for industry.[10]

The inefficiency illusion and the antiexport bias in the exchange rate system have interacted to the mutual reinforcement of both and to the hindrance of a change in policy. The inefficiency illusion reinforces the belief of policy-makers that industry is not efficient enough to export. The antiexport bias in the exchange rate structure makes exports impossible. The resultant lack of exports confirms the policy-makers' view that industry is

TABLE 5

THE "INDUSTRIAL INEFFICIENCY ILLUSION" IN BRAZIL
EXCESS OF DOMESTIC PRICE (COST) OVER INTERNATIONAL PRICE

SECTOR	AT FINANCIAL EXCHANGE RATE	AT INDUSTRIAL COST EXCHANGE RATE*
Nonmetallic minerals	40%	— 5%†
Metallurgy	34	—10
Machinery	34	—10
Electrical equipment	57	6
Transport equipment	57	6
Wood products	23	—17
Furniture	68	13
Paper and products	48	0
Rubber products	78	20
Leather products	66	12
Chemicals	34	—10
Pharmaceuticals	37	— 7
Perfumes and soaps	94	31
Plastics	48	0
Textiles	81	22
Clothing	103	37
Food products	27	—14
Beverages	83	24
Tobacco	78	20
Printing and publishing	59	7

* Derived as follows—rate for intermediate products 1.49
rate for wages 1.48
1.48

† A negative sign indicates domestic price is below international price.
SOURCE: J. Bergsman and Pedro Malan, "The Structure of Protection in Brazil" in B. Balassa, et al., *The Structure of Protection in Developing Countries* (Baltimore: Johns Hopkin Press, 1971), Tables 6.6 and 6.8.

unable to export. In view of the obvious scarcity of foreign exchange, however, the fact that it is impossible for industry to export means that additional import substitution must be undertaken. This in turn implies higher import restrictions, which cause an increase in the inefficiency illusion. As a result, the policy-makers become even more convinced of the inefficiency of industry and its inability to export, and at the same time the higher import restrictions increase the antiexport bias, making it ever less likely that industry will become foreign exchange generating.

THE LOW EMPLOYMENT GENERATION OF INDUSTRY

As we have pointed out, industry's low labor absorption is related to the underutilization of existing plant and equipment, and with multiple-shift work industrial employment would be substantially increased. An understanding of the reasons underlying the decision of most industrial firms in Latin America to use single shifts requires the resolution of the apparent paradox that while private profit maximizers find it preferable to operate three plants at one shift, from society's point of view it would appear preferable to operate one plant at three shifts, thus economizing on the scarcer resources, capital, and using labor extensively. The paradox is resolved if it is borne in mind that the private sector makes its decisions at market prices, whereas the public sector evaluates these private decisions at "social" or "shadow" prices. If market and shadow prices are sufficiently different, it is perfectly possible for the decision at private prices to lead to the installation of several factories all of which will be operated at one shift, while the same decision when evaluated at shadow prices would lead to the installation of a single factory to be operated on a multiple-shift basis. The focus of the inquiry then has to move to the causes for divergence between market and shadow prices.

The systematic distortions between private and shadow prices existing in most Latin American economies are to be seen in the following areas:

1. The price of output. Under the existing exchange rate system only the marginal revenue in the domestic market is relevant from the private point of view. Given the oligopolistic nature of many commodity markets in Latin America, each seller perceives a low demand elasticity for his sales and a marginal revenue well below the going price. From society's point of view the output is worth (potentially) the foreign exchange it would earn if exported multiplied by the shadow price of foreign exchange. This value is without exception a multiple of the privately perceived marginal revenue.

2. The price of capital goods. Most Latin American tariff structures and industrial promotion laws provide for the duty-free import of capital goods. Such a procedure implies charging the private buyer of these capital goods too little both for the scarce foreign exchange which he is using and for the scarce investment funds that he is allocating. On this count, one would expect operation to be overly capital intensive.

3. Market wage rate. In most Latin American economies, the wage rate in the industrial sector is set by a combination of industrial processes involving government wage-setting and unions. In all cases, the result is substantially above what a free labor market would produce. As a result, the market wage lies above the social marginal cost of labor, i.e., labor's shadow price. On this account, private decisions would tend toward the underutilization of labor in their operations. The impact of the wage rate goes farther, however; many times the legislation requires overtime pay for night labor, which distorts the market wage from its shadow price even more.[11] Finally, social security legislation and other fringe benefits,[12] severance pay, and firing regulations[13] may increase the cost of employing labor beyond its take-home pay and further widen the differential between the market cost of labor and its social cost.

4. Credit structure. In most Latin American economies, credit to finance installation of fixed capital is available on considerably easier terms and in larger quantities than is credit for working capital. Yet it is precisely the latter which is necessary for

the multiple-shift working of plants, since inventories of goods in process as a ratio of total capital investment increases substantially in these plants. As a result, the private production decision is biased toward excess fixed capital intensity.

5. Tax structure. In most Latin American tax legislations, the depreciation deductible from corporate income tax is based on the number of years of the life of the equipment, with no allowance made for intensity of use. As a result, second- and third-shift-originated profits are taxed at an effectively higher corporate income tax rate than are first-shift profits. This progressive corporate income tax by level of utilization is, of course, a disincentive for private decision-makers to install capital intensive multiple-shifting operations.

6. Unavailability of skilled and supervisory personnel. Skilled and supervisory labor are inputs complementary to capital, unskilled labor, and foreign exchange. The total unavailability of labor could therefore prevent any production from taking place. The extreme case of such unavailability arises in the family firm wherein the management is fully concentrated in the owner himself who, of course, cannot work twenty-four hours a day. In larger firms, with hired management, the availability problem becomes a cost problem. With this type of labor very scarce, it is obvious that its price will be high, both in the market place and in terms of its shadow wage. It is likely, however, that the market wage will be above the shadow wage even in this case, since private supply price of nighttime labor is, in part at least, a function of the lack of nighttime amenities such as transportation, security, etc. From society's point of view, if the social context is reorganized to include as a matter of course triple-shifting everywhere in the economy, these nighttime services would be available in a volume similar to the daytime level. As a consequence, the private supply price would fall. Through the interdependence of social arrangements, therefore, the shadow price of nighttime supervisory labor may well be below the market price.[14]

It may be well at this point to remember that the distortions listed will tend to lead private decision-makers to underutilize installed capacity, and indeed to plan their investments in such a way as to leave capital idle a certain proportion of the time. It does not follow, however, that the social optimum would be a twenty-four-hour-a-day operation throughout the year. Such a conclusion would require a particular configuration between the shadow costs of factors and the shadow price of output. The general arguments presented so far do not enable such a conclusion to be drawn, although it is not unlikely that upon the empirical quantification of the relevant values, round-the-clock operation throughout the year would turn out to be the social optimum in a wide range of industries.

IMPLICATIONS OF THE CONUNDRUM

The inconsistency in the growth rates of sectors using and supplying foreign exchange has important effects on the major policy problems confronting Latin American governments. The conundrum has an impact on the following four areas of policy concern: (1) balance of payments, (2) stabilization, (3) employment, and (4) distribution.

1. Balance of payments. Economic theory teaches us that a balance of payments deficit can be corrected through recourse to relative price changes and to real income changes. Price changes are usually implemented through a devaluation, which raises the price of traded goods compared to nontraded goods. As a result, a country exports more and imports less. A lower real income ensues, reinforcing the fall in the demand for imports and reducing domestic demand for exportables, thus supporting the increase in exports.

Under Latin American conditions, the price effect is virtually null for several reasons. On the import side, substitution possibilities between existing imports and domestic production are small or nonexistent, since the overwhelming proportion of imports consists of industrial raw materials which are not available domestically. Price elasticity for imports then comes primarily from substitution in final demand between commodities of different import intensity. With imports making up a small proportion of costs only, however, the price increase of imports themselves has to be substantial in order to cause the price of the commodities into which they are embodied to rise differentially. Thus even respectable own price elasticities for final goods translate into quite low elasticities for the imported components. On the other side of the balance of payments, it has been very difficult to incorporate new commodities into the export trade because of the size of the devaluation necessary to overcome the cost differential between traditional and nontraditional commodities. Indeed, devaluations of the magnitude required would be so large as to set off reactions on the part of income receivers that would rapidly nullify the devaluation. Thus any elasticity in the overall supply of exports results from increased production of traditional export products as well as from diversion to the export market of quantities destined to the home market.

The importance of the income effect for the balance of payments adjustment process is reinforced by these rigidities. With imported inputs being almost a fixed proportion of industrial output, an adjustment on the import side requires a fall in final demand, i.e. a reduction in real income. On the other hand, on the export side, a fall in real income can contribute to export revenue through reduction in the domestic consumption of exportables.

If industrial exports existed in the economy, the balance of payments adjustment process could rely much more than at present on the price effect, since in that case the supply of exports would be substantially more elastic because of the greater ease with which existing industrial products are converted into new export products.

2. Price stabilization. Traditionally, Latin American stabilizations emphasize adjustments on the demand side of the market. It is argued that if demand is reduced sufficiently, prices can no longer rise. As a result, the main policy tools traditionally used are tight money and a reduction in the government deficit. In practice this approach is often self-defeating, since lower demand

may well lead to a lower level of activity with concomitant reduction in government revenue both directly and through a lower level of trade taxes.[15] The only clear success which this approach can guarantee is an improvement in the balance of payments through the real income effect on imports.

More recently, some attention has been paid to cost push inflation originating in wages, and attempts have been made to stabilize through Phase Two type wage and price agreements. This approach has been followed in Chile[16] and Argentina.[17] In the latter case, due consideration was not given to the impact of the conundrum, since the possibility of cost increases originating from changes in the exchange rate were not built into the policy framework, and as a result not enough emphasis was given to the need to increase export earnings in order to prevent devaluation and the consequent breakup of the price-wage agreement.

The underlying problem arises from the difficulty, in the face of a balance of a payments constraint, of increasing domestic production in order to dampen price increases from the supply side of the market. Under these circumstances stability at low growth is possible, but an increased rate of growth cannot be sustained.

In the presence of industrial exports, a policy reducing domestic demand can be effectively supplemented by one increasing export demand through selective or general devaluation. Such policies could create a stabilization in total demand and improve the balance of payments by diverting supplies from the domestic market to the foreign market. At the same time, the ensuing availability of foreign exchange would allow maintenance and even expansion of domestic production with the consequent anti-inflationary impact of increased supply. Furthermore, economic growth could be accelerated with increased participation in the export market, creating the availability of foreign exchange needed for expanding supply to the domestic market and the further dampening of domestic inflationary situations.

3. Employment: There are three possible routes to the raising

of the level of employment. The first is to increase the growth of capital stock with a constant capital labor ratio. This alternative is directly affected by the conundrum, since it implies raising the growth rate and hence the required level of imports.

The second route is better use of the existing level of capital formation through investment in more labor intensive industries, i.e., change in the capital labor ratio.

This alternative does hold more promise of not being totally inhibited by the basic policy conundrum, but it is not at all certain that labor intensive technologies are also import saving. Indeed, it may well be that the opposite occurs (e.g., higher raw material wastage), in which case greater labor intensity would mean an aggravation of the growth problem.

The third alternative is more intensive use of the capital stock.

While the underutilization of labor has been recognized in Latin America for a long time, evidence on the underutilization of capital is only gradually accumulating. Not only do many of the Latin American economies periodically use installed productive capacity at levels below their own customary norm, but the norm itself is based on utilization of capital at less than 24 hours a day for 365 days a year less maintenance. While detailed information on the amount of shift work is unavailable, it appears that multiple shifting takes place primarily in the process-centered industries in which 24-hour operation is required for technical reasons. In Colombia, available data show that capital is used at about 50 percent of 24-hour capacity on the average.[18] Available data from Argentina show deviations from the usual norm of utilization to have fluctuated between 55 percent and 67 percent of this norm.

Tackling this problem, however, requires coming to grips with the basic conundrum itself. Expanding capacity utilization would have only minimal foreign exchange investment requirements, and the resulting expansion of the level of industrial output means larger imports of industrial inputs. A higher level of employment through capacity utilization is possible only if the foreign exchange availability increases, and the most plausible source of such an increase is in the sale abroad of some of the products arising from increased capacity utilization itself. But such a solution would involve making industry foreign exchange generating and therefore is identical with the solution of the basic policy conundrum.[19]

TABLE 6

ARGENTINA

UTILIZATION OF INSTALLED CAPACITY

SECTOR	PERCENTAGE OF ACTUAL OUTPUT WITH RESPECT TO MAXIMUM OUTPUT			
	1961	1963	1964	1965
Food and beverages	48.8	53.2	48.9	51.5
Tobacco	82.7	81.9	88.6	91.2
Textiles	83.2	59.2	68.9	77.1
Clothing	88.3	64.2	72.5	78.4
Wood	72.7	48.6	55.2	70.4
Paper and cardboard	55.1	48.3	52.7	62.4
Printing and publishing	73.3	58.3	62.4	70.8
Chemicals	73.4	59.9	68.1	73.8
Petroleum derivatives	87.9	78.2	84.7	83.6
Rubber	80.5	54.0	66.2	77.6
Leather	84.2	66.8	77.8	79.9
Stones, glass, and ceramics	70.2	59.0	68.7	71.8
Metals, excluding machinery	59.4	40.8	50.3	66.6
Vehicles and machinery (excluding electrical equipment	78.6	44.6	56.5	65.6
Electrical machines and equipment	59.2	43.5	47.6	61.0
Weighted average	67.2	54.6	59.5	66.1

SOURCE: CONADE, Results of the Survey on Production and Investment Expectations of Industrial Enterprises (Buenos Aires: CONADE, March 1965), Table 3.

4. Distribution. Changes in the regional and personal distribution of income as well as changes in the income shares of the public and private sectors are an increasingly important policy goal for Latin American governments. In addition to the greater difficulty of achieving such readjustments under the conditions of relatively slow growth forced upon the economy by the continuation of the basic conundrum, there are some direct connections between the sources and uses of foreign exchange and the

possibility of executing a successful redistribution policy. One major connection runs from the exchange rate to export prices and to the income of exporters as compared to urban laborers. This is most obviously the case if wage goods are also the country's primary export products. If the exchange rate goes up, agricultural producers get higher incomes and the cost of living rises.[20] If agriculture is in the hands of large landowners, this will mean a negative redistribution of income, although it may at the same time be a necessary adjustment in the incentives to provide foreign exchange. The distributional policy clashes directly with the balance of payments policy. If industrial exports existed, a balance of payments policy could accommodate a lower increase in prices for farmers, increasing instead the foreign exchange earned by industry.

On the other hand, a reorganization of land tenure, or the institutionalization of worker participation in management of the mines or indeed of government participation in mining, or the merchandising of export products, may lead for a time at least to some disorganization, lower productivity, and lower value of exports; contraction in the rest of the economy and reduction rather than redistribution of everybody's income would result. Were industry foreign exchange producing rather than foreign exchange using, adjustments of an organizational nature in the primary sectors would be much more bearable, since the economy would be able to compensate a short fall of earnings from these sectors through an increased amount of industrial exporting.

GENERATING FOREIGN EXCHANGE FROM INDUSTRIAL PRODUCTION

The basic policy conundrum will be solved only when industry becomes foreign exchange generating as well as foreign exchange using. Two necessary conditions for such a conversion are price competitiveness of industrial output in the world market and the availability of marketing channels.[21]

Price competitiveness

The achievement of price competitiveness requires a modification in the exchange rate system. Two techniques are available for this: compensated devaluation and export subsidies.

A compensated devaluation is one in which simultaneous and offsetting adjustments are undertaken in the financial exchange rate and in the trade restrictions such that all the commodity exchange rates for imports and traditional exports stay unchanged, the only net change taking place in the financial rate and in the nontraditional export rate. As a result, nontraditional exports obtain the equivalent of a subsidy. An example can be given with the Argentinian exchange rate system cited earlier.[22]

Precompensated Devaluation				Postcompensated Devaluation		
TOTAL	TAX/SUBSIDY	BASIC	RATE	BASIC	TAX/SUBSIDY	TOTAL
200	— 10%	220	Agricultural Exports	330	— 40%	200
220	0	220	Financial	330	0	330
260	+ 18%	220	Nontraditional Exports	330	+ 18%	390
330	+ 50%	220	Raw Material Imports	330	0	330
460	+120%	220	Semimanufactured Imports	330	+ 47%.	460
600	+175%	220	Component Imports	330	+ 80%	600
700	+220%	220	Finished Product Imports	330	+115%	700

Inspection will show that with a compensated devaluation, the exchange rate for nontraditional exports has had a real increase of 50 percent in comparison with the remainder of the rates; it is much closer now to the industrial cost rates, and exceeds the raw material imports rate.

The export subsidy directly affects the commodity exchange rate for nontraditional exports and therefore eliminates the preexisting bias. If the export subsidy is given across the board as a fixed percentage of the FOB value of exports, its administration is extremely simple.

The main objection to export subsidies arises from the supposed fiscal cost. It is argued that such subsidies, if successful, imply substantial disbursements from the treasury which, under the stringent fiscal conditions in Latin America, are better used elsewhere. This objection is not generally valid, however. If the subsidy program is successful and exports take a place under it, additional economic activity would result which in itself and through the foreign trade multiplier would generate a substantial increase in the tax base. This increase in the base would generate additional revenue for the exchequer. The new revenue would then serve to cover in part or in whole the subsidy necessary to generate the exports in the first place. In this manner, through a combined foreign trade and fiscal multiplier, export subsidies generate their own (partial or total) financing. Under the Latin American conditions in which the marginal import propensities are rather low, foreign trade tax multipliers tend to be high, and as a result fairly large export subsidies can be supported by the revenue generated in this form, particularly if they are paid only to new exports. In essence, such a view of the fiscal impact of export subsidization implies the use of a full capacity utilization budget. This full capacity utilization budget is analogous to the full employment budget introduced recently in the United States. The difference is that in the United States version an expenditure by government or a reduction of revenue will generate domestic activity and additional domestic employment, which will in turn finance the change in the fiscal situation. In Latin America it is the expenditure of public funds for the creation of exports that generates a higher level of economic activity and therefore an increase in revenue.

A simple model of the following kind allows the calculation of a full utilization budget and specifically the maximal subsidy payable without net fiscal costs to the exchequer.

Define:

P = total expenditure of the private sector
p = marginal propensity to spend of the private sector
M = imports at CIF prices
m = marginal (= average) propensity to import

Y = income at market prices
E = exports at FOB prices
G = government expenditure
T = fiscal revenue
a = rate of ad valorem import duties
td = rate of direct taxes on income
ti = rate of taxation on domestic transactions expressed as a percentage of national income

Then:

$$P = po + p(1 - td - ti - a\frac{M}{Y})Y \qquad (1)$$

$$M(1+a) = m(1 - td - ti - a\frac{M}{Y})Y \qquad (2)$$

$$E = E_0 \qquad (3)$$
$$G = G_0 \qquad (4)$$
$$Y = P + G + (E - M) \qquad (5)$$
$$T = aM + (td + ti)Y \qquad (6)$$

This system of equations tells us that gross private disposable income[23] determines the level of final demand for domestic goods and for imports measured in domestic prices (eqq[1 and 2]), that exports and government expenditure are exogenously determined (eqq[3 and 4]), that income must equal expenditure (eq 5), and that fiscal revenue comes from several kinds of taxes.

The total differential of fiscal revenue with regard to income from exports will show the net increase in fiscal resources per peso of additional income of exporters.

$$dT = \frac{am(1 - tx) + (1+a)(td + ti)}{(1+a)\ [1 - (1 - tx)[p - m/(1+a)]\ ]} \qquad (7)$$

where $tx = td + ti + a\frac{M}{Y}$

Incorporating export subsidies explicitly requires substituting E by $E^* = (1+s)E$, where s = rate of subsidy on FOB value of exports. The net fiscal change after export subsidy payments can now be written as

$$dTn=\frac{am(1-tx)+(1+a)(td+ti)}{(1+a)\ \{1-(1-tx)[p-m/(1+a)]\ \}}\ dE^{*}-\frac{s}{1+s}dE^{*} \quad (8)$$

Applying these formulae to Argentina with tx=.43; td=.0467; ti=.07; a=.024; m=.159, p=1, one obtains

$$dTn=.566\ dE^{*}-\frac{s}{1+s}dE^{*} \quad (9)$$

To obtain the maximal subsidy rate, s, which causes no net deficit, equation (9) is set equal to zero and s = 1.3 which means that in Argentina a subsidy rate of up to 130 percent of the FOB value of the export will not disimprove the fiscal balance.[24] Other countries will surely have different and probably lower cutoff points, but economies as close as the Latin American ones cannot fail to have high foreign trade multipliers and hence room for substantial export subsidization without a negative net fiscal impact.

An estimate of the excess of costs of production over prices in developed countries, and hence of the subsidies required for export competitiveness in Brazil, Chile, and Mexico on the assumption of fully competitive markets all around and no excess capacity, is shown in Table 6. These figures overestimate the true price/cost gap to the extent that exports are additional to, rather than substitutes for, domestic sales, and that excess capacity exists; marginal cost may then well be below the average cost of the domestic market. A similar offset would come from monopolistic pricing in the domestic commodity markets of potential Latin American export products, which would also imply marginal cost below price. Finally, monopolistic pricing in developed countries by producers of potential Latin American export products would also generate an offset by providing a higher price floor which must be undercut.

If the compensated devaluation and an export subsidy yielding precisely the same commodity exchange rates were compared, the following differences would emerge:

1. Under compensated devaluation, the financial exchange rate

has been raised, whereas this does not take place under a subsidy program. This modification implies a net loss (gain) in wealth for all individuals and firms in the domestic economy with net foreign liabilities (assets). Also implied is a reduction in the expected profitability of foreign private investors.[25]

2. The fiscal impact of the new exports will be identical under both systems. However, the shift in tax base under the compensated devaluation is likely to produce an increase in revenue if the balance of trade was initially in surplus, and a decrease in revenue if it was initially in deficit.

In most real world cases, the adoption of a compensated devaluation would produce a somewhat different structure of exchange rates than would result from the adoption of an export subsidy program. The main difference would arise from the impossibility of fully compensating the devaluation on the import side, since some tariffs will initially have been below the level of the desired export subsidy equivalent for nontraditional exports. As a result, some increase in import commodity exchange rates will take place, albeit at the lower end of the spectrum. As a result, compensated devaluation will have a slightly higher tax yield, and a small increase in price as well as perhaps a slightly weaker net export incentive, if the nontraditional exports are heavy users of the commodities whose import exchange rate has been raised.

In choosing between these two alternative policies, additional consideration must be given to some factors that, though not fundamentally economic in nature, are nonetheless very important. These are the following:

1. The effect on the inefficiency illusion in industry. Compensated devaluation, through its modification of the financial exchange rate, affects the inefficiency illusion, reducing it proportionately to the change in that financial exchange rate. The export subsidy program has no effect whatsoever on the inefficiency illusion.

2. The national commitments regarding export subsidies. Under GATT rules, an explicit subsidy may well be illegal, whereas

a compensated devaluation falls outside GATT rules and into the IMF rules under which it is perfectly acceptable; indeed, it is regarded as liberalization and therefore "good." This difference is less definitive than it might seem, however, since tax refunds have repeatedly been accepted by the GATT and it is very hard to distinguish in practice between the tax refund and an explicit export subsidy.

3. The apparent distribution of the tax burden. Under compensated devaluation, traditional exporters seem to be paying a substantial export tax. As a result, charges of discrimination against the goose that produces the golden egg of foreign exchange may well be levied. On the other hand, the explicit export subsidy policy may well appear a giveaway program to industrialists, and the charge will be levied that the high income groups are milking the tax system.

Marketing Channels

Marketing channels are as necessary as price competitiveness if industry is to become rapidly foreign exchange generating. It is useful in this context to divide potential export commodities into two kinds: (a) standardized commodities, and (b) differentiated commodities. Into the first group fall items such as steel and chemicals which are sold on a specification basis and which have highly competitive international markets. In these, the marketing problem is no different from the price competitiveness problem. Any preexisting import house can become an export house and sell standardized commodities on the world market by simply having an attractive quotation. Price is everything, and quality is easily determined, with standard rebates existing for quality differences. In the case of standardized commodities, therefore, the existence of price competitiveness alone will very soon generate the necessary marketing channels.

The marketing problem for nonstandardized commodities is much more complex, since it is in these that brands, user preferences, and product quality are important elements. For the marketing of this type of product, the multinational enterprise offers a unique potential, since it controls internally a very substantial market and is able to monitor quality and guarantee performance worldwide. Governments interested in stimulating the establishment of marketing channels, therefore, are well advised to look into the possible conversion of the production facilities of multinational enterprises within their jurisdictions from foreign exchange users to foreign exchange producers.[26]

GENERATING INDUSTRIAL EMPLOYMENT

The industrial sectors of Latin America will become significant contributors to the solution of the Latin American unemployment problems only if the rate of capacity utilization is increased substantially. If such an increase occurs, it should be possible to achieve at a minimum a doubling of industrial employment.

Increased capacity utilization in conjunction with a high rate of growth requires a substantial expansion of the market for Latin American industrial products. On the other hand, an increased capacity utilizaton with a high level of industrial output also requires a greater availability of foreign exchange to pay for the imported inputs. A convenient way of solving both these problems simultaneously consists of routing a part of the additional output onto the foreign market and in the process earning the foreign exchange necessary to acquire the imported inputs.

In policy terms, the generation of industrial exports in order to utilize capacity is no different from the generation of industrial exports for any other purpose. Therefore, the policies outlined in the previous section are directly applicable.

In addition to making a market available, it is necessary to go at least some part of the way toward correcting the distortions which exist in factor prices. The main element in this instance may be the high cost of labor, which exceeds the shadow wage by a considerable extent. This is an item which is very difficult to affect by policy precisely because of its magnitude; i.e., the theoretically desirable wage subsidies are simply not fiscally feasible. It is therefore necessary to look to the other cost-distorting elements for an improvement.

The cost of capital goods can be affected rather easily through an increase in the import tariff on these items. Such a policy change would bring the ratio of the prices of capital goods and labor closer to the ratio of their shadow prices and thus is likely to lead private decisions on the scaling and utilization of plant to conform more closely to the socially optimal level. Furthermore, rules governing depreciation should be amended in order to allow depreciation for the use of capital equipment to vary as a function of utilization. In this way, the progressive taxation by level of utilization existing at present would be eliminated, and the incentive to single shift in multiple plants would be reduced accordingly.

Finally, special lending programs in which funds would be made available as working capital for the utilization of plant and equipment, rather than for its installation, would provide a substantial antidistorting measure in the capital market. Such an innovation of lending for capital use would, however, constitute an important departure from existing practice in which lending against the real security of the machine is extremely common, and in which borrowers are expected to provide the major part of their working capital.

It should be noted that a full-fledged capacity utilization program requires that the existence of some externalities in the multiple-shifting decisions of different plants be recognized. These externalities arise as a result of the requirements of night workers for social services such as transportation, electricity, resturants, etc. Consequently, a synchronized plan in which numerous plants convert to multiple shifting at the same time may well be socially more efficient and easier to accomplish than the piecemeal transition to multiple shifting of individual plants.

CONTRIBUTIONS OF TRADE POLICY TO LATIN AMERICAN ECONOMIC GROWTH

In the foregoing it has been argued that the basic conundrum of Latin American economic growth arises out of the foreign exchange using nature of its industry. Unless the industrial sector becomes foreign exchange producing, it can no longer function as a leading sector and act as the engine of growth for the whole economy.

Similarly, the industrial sector has not provided the expected solution to the unemployment problem, largely because of the low level of capacity utilization which is prevalent in Latin America.

The foreign exchange using nature of industry is in large measure the result of policy. The exchange rate system is structured in such a way as implicitly to tax industrial exports while creating at the same time an industrial inefficiency illusion.

The low level of capacity utilization is policy induced as well. Government policy has generated distortions by creating deviations between the market price and the corresponding shadow price of production for export, and by legislating higher effective corporation rates on profit from the second and third shifts of operation. At the same time, government has tolerated discrimination in lending in favor of fixed investment and against working capital.

The basic policy conundrum drastically limits the possibility of success in obtaining the major policy targets of increased growth, increased employment, greater price stability, and more equitable distribution. Whereas conventional devaluation is inappropriate to deal with the conundrum, either a compensated devaluation or a system of export subsidies is likely to be effective. These policies will make it possible to place the output from additional capacity utilization in industry and earn foreign exchange needed to pay for the imported inputs required to sustain such higher levels of utilization. Full capacity utilization requires, however, additional policies centering mainly on an increase in the price of capital goods imports, the lending for capacity utilization, and the taxation of profits from different shifts of operation.

Thus international trade policy can be said to lie at the heart of the development prospects for the region. One must now look to policy-makers to recognize increasingly the conundrum as well as the quasi-Keynesian situation in the labor market. Once these have been adequately recognized and diagnosed, the appropriate policies can follow.

Notes

RESEARCH SUPPORT from the Development Advisory Service, Harvard University, is gratefully acknowledged.

1. Werner Baer, "The Inflation Controversy in Latin America: A Survey," *Latin American Research Review* 2 (Winter 1967).

2. Marcelo Diamand, "Seis Falsos Dilemas en el Debate Economico Nacional," Cuadernos del Centro de Estudios Industriales No. 5 (Buenos Aires, 1971), pp. 50-53.

3. The Peruvian fishmeal industry is the exception. Yet even it consisted of a manufacturing as well as a primary part.

4. For a discussion of the effect of changes in the composition of demand, see David Felix, "The Dilemma of Import Substitution—Argentina," in *Development Policy: Theory and Practice*, ed. G. F. Papanek (Cambridge: Harvard University Press, 1968).

5. Werner Baer and Michel E. A. Herve, "Employment and Industrialization in Developing Countries," *Quarterly Journal of Economics* 80 (February 1966).

6. Daniel Schydlowsky, "Fiscal Policy for Full Capacity Industrial Growth in Latin America," presented at the 21st Annual Latin American Conference, University of Florida, February, 1971, Economic Development Report No. 201, Center for International Affairs, Harvard University, 1971.

7. The most general case arises when the same commodity has different import rates; preferential import and export regimes differentiate rates even further.

8. Taken from CARTTA (Camera Argentina de Radio, Television, Telecomunicaciones y Afines), "Proyecto de Modificacion de la Estructura Arancelario-Cambiaria" (September 1966).

9. w=Marginal physical product (MPP) x price of output. If the unit of output is set at an amount costing $1 CIF, then we have w=marginal physical product x average commodity exchange rate for output.

10. Note that for a more accurate calculation each sector's costs should be converted at that sector's cost exchange rate. If this were done, the numbers in the second column would change once again. The general result would not, however, be negated.

11. Note that the premium for night labor may be exactly "right"; i.e., it may reflect accurately the social disutility of night work. Nonetheless, night pay may exceed the night shadow wage (just as the day wage exceeds its shadow wage).

12. The magnitude of the fringe benefits is considerable. Ferrero (R. A. Ferrero and A. J. Altmeyer, *Estudio Economico de la Legislacion Social Peruana y Sugerencias para su Mejoramiento* [Lima, 1957]) found them to be 45 percent of wages in Peru, while Gregory (Peter Gregory, *Industrial Wages in Chile* [Ithaca: Cornell University Press, 1967]) found them to be about 100 percent of on-the-job earnings in Chile.

13. For a discussion of labor force hiring as a fixed investment, see Raymond Vernon, "Organization as a Scale Factor in the Growth of Firms," in J. Markham and G. F. Papanek, eds., *Industrial Organization and Industrial Development* (Boston: Houghton Mifflin, 1970).

14. I owe this point to Dr. Stephen Guisinger.

15. For an empirical estimate of tax multipliers in a quasi-Keynesian situation see Daniel Schydlowsky, "Short Run Employment Policy in Semi-Industrialized Economies," Economic Development Report No. 73, Center for International Affairs, Harvard University, *Economic Development and Cultural Change* (April 1971).

16. Jorge Cauas, "Stabilization Policy—The Chilean Case," *Journal of Political Economy*, July/August 1970, pp. 815-25.

17. IDES (Instituto de Desarrollo Economico y Social), *Situacion Actual y Perspectivas de la Economia Argentina*, April 1967; April 1968.

18. Francisco Thoumi, "Industrial Capacity Utilization in Colombia: Some Empirical Findings," mimeographed, 1972.

19. For a more complete discussion, see Schydlowsky, "Fiscal Policy for Full Capacity Industrial Growth."

20. The same distributional effects obtain even if the export products are not wage goods. In that case, devaluation will increase export earnings and reduce the real wage via price increases of importables.

21. These two conditions may not, however, be sufficient in themselves. In addition, quality of product, regularity of supply, minimum quantity, and other elements may be required.

22. CARTTA, "Proyecto de Modificacion."

23. Note that this is defined at factor cost—hence the terms for indirect taxation and import duties.

24. For more detail on this model including period analysis, sectoral disaggregation, and sensitivity analysis of the parameters, see Schydlowsky, "Short Run Employment Policy."

25. New foreign investors will find offsetting effects: (a) their dollar capital expenditure goes down in so far as they purchase nontraded goods and domestic labor; and (b) the dollar repatriation value of their profit stream will be reduced proportionately to the devaluation. Unless the capital expenditure is totally in the local currency, the result will be reduced profitability for a given size operation. Foreign investors may, however, find ample compensation from the higher growth rate attendant upon a successful compensated devaluation. For a discussion of devaluation as perceived by the foreign investor see Raymond Vernon, *Manager in the International Economy* (New York: Prentice-Hall, 1968), pp. 54 ff.

26. Mexico and more recently Brazil have used this technique successfully.

ANTONIO CARILLO-FLORES

Trade Policies And Latin American Development

AT THIS MOMENT, Latin America is undergoing a period of the greatest political and economic diversity in its history. New systems are being tried out, some of them already familiar in other areas of the world, others peculiar to our hemisphere. More than ever before, social structures are subject to criticism. Many traditional ideas have been abandoned. All this has been occurring against the background of one permanent fact, namely, that tremendous differences in territory, resources, and population exist among the various countries of the area. Thus, we can readily realize that, if it has always been difficult to make assertions that might be valid for all Latin America, it is even more difficult to do so now.

Recently a prominent English banker said to me, "The countries of the subcontinent will begin to come out ahead when they stop talking about 'Latin America.' Latin America simply does not exist." But on the other hand, the 1967 meeting at Punta del Este coined a definition entirely different from those formulated in the nineteenth century. Latin America, it was said, is made up of countries on this continent that are in the process of development, independent of their history, their language, and their population characteristics. With this definition, of course, Latin America covers the whole hemisphere, with the exception of the United States and Canada.

I believe that in the last decade Latin America has manifested its existence in very positive and valuable ways. For the first time in a century and a half, the traditional historical solidarity of Latin America—and here I refer to the Spanish—and Portuguese-speaking peoples—a solidarity that was rhetorical and nostalgic for the most part, has been undergoing a change into something more promising and more fertile, even though that fertility may be but that of a seed. A new type of nationalism has been born—a Latin American nationalism which reached its high point in the Declaration of American Presidents in 1967, when the presidents made the bold decision to create a common market. It is certainly true that the difficulties encountered in carrying out that decision have been appreciably greater than one could have foreseen. But the goal has already been fixed, and it *will not* be abandoned. The goal will not be abandoned because, except for Argentina, Brazil, and Mexico, it is extremely improbable that the countries in the area will be able to achieve the development they so eagerly seek—especially in the field of industrialization with its consequent raising of the level of life for their peoples—without integrating themselves into larger economic areas.

But until the goal set forth at the Punta del Este Conference is accomplished—and I doubt that this will occur during this century—commercial or investment policies in Argentina, Brazil, or Mexico raise completely different problems from those faced by any of the other Latin American countries. Even among these three major countries, vast differences exist. How can Mexican commercial policies be the same as Argentina's, when we consider that approximately 70 percent of Mexico's trade is carried on with the United States, while in 1968 Argentina's trade with the United States amounted to only some 12 percent of its total sales?

Nevertheless, some ideas are gradually taking shape as a common patrimony among all the Latin American countries, big and small. Among these ideas is the ever deepening conviction that limiting themselves to being exporters only of raw materials will never give them access to those resources that an acceptable development demands.

If, in general, it is difficult for the developing countries to compete in the world markets with their manufactured products, it would be fair if they were granted some kind of priority for the export of primary goods. The Williams Commission, in its report to President Nixon in July, 1971, supports this idea in a limited way. It recommends "reducing incentives for non-competitive production, as, for example, in rice and perhaps cotton." Mexico naturally welcomes this suggestion.

Even without the technical precision that is possible today, this concept was expressed at the 1945 Chapultepec Conference, which, it should be remembered, took place *before* the end of World War II. And it was reiterated at the Bogotá Conference of 1948, at which time the Organization of American States was created. During that same conference, our countries insisted on the necessity of creating a bank specifically dedicated to serving the developmental needs of Latin America. At that same time, the Andean countries brought up the matter of preferential trade treatment among themselves, thus setting the precedent for regional integration.

At that time the United States, committed as it was to the gigantic task of reconstructing Europe, gave no encouragement to the Latin American proposals. Its fundamentally negative attitude lasted practically all through the 1950s. The Export-Import Bank, to the extent of its possibilities, continued its meritorious task of granting credit for the purpose of development; and after a rather vacillating beginning, the World Bank began to lend its support to some infrastructure projects. But no progress was made in the vital area of commerce, even though it was recognized that many of the trade problems were of worldwide character. Among them, however, there were some in which regional action was possible.

It took several years to overcome the frustrations that resulted from the Bogotá Conference, aggravated later by those in Quintandiña in 1954 and in Buenos Aires in 1957. The latter was the first formal conference of American states dedicated to economic questions. During those meetings, a basic discrepancy became evident: the position of the United States, based on its own experiences, was that the furthering of economic development was primarily the function of private capital, and that if Latin America wished to receive foreign financial assistance, it should first create what was called a favorable climate for those investments. Facing that postulation, many Latin American countries, without failing to recognize the significant importance of private capital in the task of development, held to the opinion that the state had unavoidable responsibilities in planning, in building up the infrastructure of its economies, and even in the creation of some basic industries. Besides, even supposing that investors were inclined to enter the scene, many historical experiences made it politically impossible to leave the domination of the weak economies of the regions in the hands of private foreign capital.

At the beginning of the 1960s, when many signs of social unrest had already appeared, and when the Cuban Revolution had produced the first socialist state in Latin America, there were some positive changes in the outlook of inter-American relations. The United States materially and politically supported the creation of the Inter-American Bank; the coffee agreement was negotiated and established; the 1960 Act of Bogotá was approved, at which time the United States recognized the necessity of cooperating with those countries that had undertaken the renovation of their social and economic structures; and finally, President Kennedy proposed the Alliance for Progress. On the other hand, Latin American aspirations toward integration began to take form.

On the world scene, the first development decade was launched with very ambitious objectives in regard to the transference of resources from the industrialized areas to the poor ones. The 1964 United Nations Conference on Trade and Development brought into focus the common hopes of the so-called Third World, and recognition was given to the necessity for a system of preferential trade treatment in favor of the developing countries. Some progress was made, but much less than had been hoped for. The gap between the rich and the poor peoples continued to widen.

Perhaps at least in part because of the frustrations of the postwar period, economic nationalism became accentuated everywhere in the world, though in Latin America it went hand in hand with the cause of integration. State responsibility toward development broadened, and with it, as a general rule, a certain preference for long-term development credits over direct private investment as the best road to international financial cooperation. At the same time, preference was shown toward multilateral over bilateral financing, as well as an ever increasing demand for so-called "soft loans." Regionally, this was handled through the Inter-American Bank, while on a worldwide scale it gave rise to the International Development Association.

The Inter-American Bank has undoubtedly fulfilled an important mission; similarly, it would be unjust to deny that, in their respective areas, the worldwide financial agencies have also been useful. As for the role in which the Latin American countries have placed private foreign capital as an auxiliary lever in their development, I believe that very little can be validly said. The majority of these countries do not fail to recognize the utility of private foreign capital, but they are convinced that it can no longer be accepted as it was in the past. Mexico has recognized this since 1917 in its Constitution, which embodied the postulates of the Mexican Revolution.

It was stated at the Conference of Presidents in Punta del Este that no Latin American country could accept the concept that the common market, which the presidents so ardently desired to establish, should come to mean the creation, under privileged conditions, of new affiliates of the big European, or Japanese, or United States industrial corporations. The presidents emphasized that it was necessary to encourage and strengthen "Latin American enterprise."

From another angle, after the excessive hopes raised by the

Alliance for Progress, Latin America came to the realization that public foreign capital in the form of credit would not be available in quantities sufficient to correct the existent insufficiency of domestic savings. This conviction lies at the root of their insistence on seeking preferential trade treatment from the rich nations in the world. The great majority of opinions expressed in Latin America have been against preferential treatment conceded by bilateral agreements with the United States. It is believed—and with good reason—that preferential treatment under such circumstances would lead to an unacceptable political subordination, precisely at the moment in the history of our area when it wants to strengthen and expand its contacts with the rest of the world.

In 1967, the United States announced that it was sympathetically studying the matter of preferential trade treatment, and as an immediate measure it decided *not* to establish any new restrictions against Latin American trade. More recently, during February, 1971, President Nixon presented to Congress his projection of United States foreign policy for the 1970s. It included a program which sought to improve hemispheric relations, which, he conceded, he had found to be at a very low level:

> We proposed a liberal system of tariff preferences for exports of the developing countries. The low-income countries need increased export earnings to finance the imports they need for development. They need improved access for their products to the massive markets of the industrialized nations. Such export increases must come largely in manufactured goods, since the demand for most primary commodities—their traditional export—grows relatively slowly. And these countries are at early stages of industrialization, so they face major hurdles in competing with the industrialized countries for sales of manufactured goods. Against this background, we proposed that all industrialized nations eliminate their tariffs on most manufactured products exported to them by all developing countries. Such preferential treatment would free an important and rapidly growing part of the trade between these two groups of nations. It would therefore provide an important new impetus to world economic development.

When President Nixon set forth that policy, problem of balance of payments had already entered an acute phase for the United States. Latin America was aware of those problems. But Latin America was also aware of the fact that not only was it in no way the cause of the problems, but it had in no way contributed to them, since the United States has always enjoyed a favorable balance of trade with our area.

We know that we must continue our struggle to increase our trade with other areas of the world, including the socialist countries. It is of great importance to us that the United States' system of preferences shall begin to operate. As was pointed out in Panama by the Mexican representative, the nations of the European Economic Community and Japan have conditioned their granting of preferential trade treatment to that of the United States.

We know that we must strengthen our internal market. And as far as Mexico in particular is concerned, we know that the income derived from the tourist trade and from the retired people who reside in Mexico places us in a more favorable position than that of the other Latin American countries. On the other hand, the physical proximity to the most powerful economic area in the world affects Mexico's trade in such a way—and as I have said, 70 percent of our trade is with the United States—that any restriction imposed on our exports to the United States perforce results in problems of an extremely serious nature.

Mexico has financed its own development to the extent of 90 percent, which is derived from internal resources. The other 10 percent has come primarily from foreign development credit plus, to a lesser degree, private foreign investments. We have zealously complied with our international foreign obligations, and we have enjoyed eighteen years of absolute monetary stability and free exchange. These are achievements without precedent in Latin America during this century.

Nationalism, which, in many areas has assumed vigorous, and at times even passionate manifestations, has existed in Mexico for more than half a century, and has had a significant influence on our social, political, and economic life. Until 1941, it created serious international problems for us. But since then, three generations of Mexicans have devised formulae which *affirm* that nationalism when it becomes essential to maintain our identity and our sovereignty, but without creating obstacles to our economic progress. Our demographic expansion, which is proceeding at a very rapid rate, obligates us to investments that will maintain our rate of development at a figure above 6 percent annually. For purposes of self-interest, this in turn makes it mandatory that we carry on our foreign economic relations with extreme care.

Not only have we complied with the mandates of our Constitution of 1917 regarding nationalization of the petroleum industry and agrarian reform, but with those regarding the nationalization of our railroads and the production of electrical energy as well. Furthermore, we follow the policy of "Mexicanizing" many other fundamental fields, such as mining, the banking system, insurance, and some basic industries. But in amicably resolving our old controversies with the United States, when we have resorted to nationalization, or to Mexicanization, this has always been done through honorable agreements with the foreign investors. The *New York Times* acknowledged the truth of this not long ago.

The bitter experiences of fifty years ago changed Mexico into a pragmatic and realistic nation, without, however, our forgetting any of the principles for which our forefathers fought. As for the specific topic of private foreign investments, our present policy is well known. Foreign investment interests us when it is associated, on a minority basis, with Mexicans, and if it brings with it new production techniques, or if it leads to national production of goods that will replace imports or increase exports. We are not interested in foreign investment if its only purpose is to try to acquire already established enterprises. This stated policy, though, has not prevented private foreign investments from showing a constantly increasing rhythm over the past twenty-five years.

It would be somewhat less than honest on my part, however, not to mention that in certain sectors there is the concern that in view of more restrictive policies in some other countries of Latin America, private foreign investment in Mexico might grow at an inconvenient rate because of excessive acceleration, particularly in the fields of manufacturing and trade.

The administrations that have successively headed the Mexican government have been attentive to these fears, trying to make sure that the most important activities in our economy remain under the control of Mexicans. But on the basis of patriotic pragmatism, the door has not been closed to foreign investment in those areas in which our own resources are insufficient to contribute to our development.

The most recent example of this is a decree issued by President Echeverría in April, 1971. This decree opened the way to the development of new tourist centers without incurring the possibility of violating our Constitution. The infrastructure—that is, the planning of the new zones—is to be undertaken by the government with the aid of international credit, but investments are to be complemented by the input of national and foreign private capital.

If there were some advice that I could offer, it would be that the foreigner should take care not to offend the Mexican sensibilities which, for historical reasons, are very susceptible, although normally they are manifested in a cordial fashion. It would not be acceptable, for instance, that tourist resorts take on the appearance of foreign enclaves in our territory.

Regarding new industrial undertakings, I should like to repeat the opinion that I customarily gave to those who sought my advice during my happy years as ambassador in Washington: within the tenets of our well-known policy, Mexico has always looked favorably toward the creation of business enterprises that would bring us new technological developments, that would increase employment, and that would constitute additional sources of government revenue. These are the things we need to raise the level of life of our people. Because of the complex nature of the problems of foreign investment and the need to avoid repetition of past conflicts, the best form of investment is that which is made openly and aboveboard, the investor setting all the facts clearly and frankly before the appropriate authorities. It is not enough that one lawyer or another express an opinion that a given investment is not prohibited. It is to the interest of the potential investor to assure himself that the Mexican government considers his proposed investment convenient. There is nothing worse for everyone involved than to try to establish an operation surreptitiously, or to use a Mexican national as a front man. By so doing, the foreign investor may even find himself exposed to the danger of losing his investment.

I should like to conclude with an observation that is broader in character. It appears that the foreign policy of the United States is now following a realistic and healthy path and is more and more freeing itself from ideological ties and outdated political concepts. This observation is drawn from the clear and ample statements made by President Nixon in the February, 1970 document previously cited, as well as from his new attitude toward China and from the measures he announced on August 15.

The relations between the United States and Latin America will become easier and friendlier in the immediate future if, within the same realistic framework, this great nation accepts the fact that the major problems in our area—some of them of tremendous proportions—have little to do with the forms the Latin American countries choose in their capital formation or in their economic planning. Rather, their choices are based on the anxious, and at times desperate need of their peoples to attain better levels of life by organizing more modern and less unjust social structures.

It is the responsibility of each Latin American nation to face its own problems. This is precisely what Mexico has been doing since 1917. And now the majority of the other Latin American countries are trying to do the same thing by exploring a wide diversity of roads. Amidst that diversity there is one common denominator: the affirmation of their independence. I do not believe that the United States will be able to exert influence on the course that each of the Latin American countries may choose to follow. On the other hand, if the United States is willing to cooperate, the changes that may occur in the political, social, and economic structures need not preclude the nations' living together in a spirit of friendship in the hemisphere.

This leads us to the real, but at the same time symbolic, importance of the 10 percent surtax on our exports.* I am sure that we Latin Americans recognize the right of the United States to have adopted this measure, among others, for the defense of its economy.

It is Mexico's desire that the U.S. program prove successful, because we know from experience that our own development becomes much more difficult when the American economy is weakened or suffers a reverse.

If, in Panama, in Bogotá, and in Washington, we have unanimously and vigorously opposed the surtax, it is because we believe that Latin America neither caused nor contributed to the lack of equilibrium in the United States balance of payments, and because our area could have been exempted without prejudicing the efficacy of the economic program. It is true that to exempt Latin America from the surtax would have been discriminatory, as your secretary of the treasury has stated. But in this year of 1971, it is accepted by all that in the area of commerce the more powerful countries can, and even should, discriminate in favor of the weaker countries. None of the arguments on the part of the United States in regard to Japan or Western Europe would have been weakened if the 10 percent surtax had not been applied to us.

As a man who has actively participated in affairs of state between Mexico and the United States for more than twenty years, I am sure that this problem, like others that have come up in the past, will be resolved. And when this happens—as I am sure

* Editor's note: this address was delivered just prior to the termination of the 10 percent surtax by the United States in December, 1971.

it will soon—all people of good will, both to the north and to the south of the Rio Grande, will continue to make every effort to strengthen the friendship which, on the basis of geography, on the basis of reciprocal interests, and on the basis of common ideals, should be maintained between the two Americas.

Name Index

Subject Index